Figure Drawing

Figure Drawing

A practical manual for all students of art

John Raynes

Hamlyn
London·New York·Sydney·Toronto

Published by
The Hamlyn Publishing Group Limited
London · New York · Sydney · Toronto
Astronaut House, Feltham, Middlesex, England

ISBN 0 600 34206 9 hardcover
ISBN 0 600 34258 1 softcover

Printed in Great Britain

The drawings in this book are the work of the author
with the exception of the dot drawings on pages 83, 113, 114
and the etching on page 86
which are the work of Polly Raynes.

Contents

Introduction

Drawing can be one of several different things.

It can be a representation of visual imagery existing only in the imagination or in dreams.

It can be the intuitive making of abstract shapes with no attempt to produce anything recognizable as observable reality.

It can be plans and sections of known or visualized objects, as by an architect or a technical draughtsman, which explain unseen internal workings and structure.

It can also be the making of images drawn from direct observation, with the intention of representing what is seen. In this type of drawing an attempt is made to discover the essential appearance of an object by close study, which is not to say that the knowledge so gained may not feed the imagination with images which can later find their way into more creative work.

This last is known as *objective* drawing, and it is with this approach to drawing that I am primarily concerned in this book.

Even within this one area of specifically objective drawing, there is an immense variety of ways of seeing: the same object can be seen and drawn in many ways, each just as 'real' and true as the others.

The earliest drawings known are those on the walls of the cave dwellings of our prehistoric ancestors. They are often, perhaps surprisingly, beautiful to our modern eyes, and they are nearly always accurate depictions of the shape of the animals then living. Early man's survival depended on these animals and it was important that they should be recognized and identified quickly and accurately. The cave artists' concentration on linear outline drawings of the animals, filled-in silhouettes in some cases, show just the information that is needed to identify an animal at a distance. Colour, markings and even some suggestion of form are there too, but above all they are accurate outline drawings.

To represent and recognize a solid three-dimensional object by linear outline was already a huge intellectual leap to have made. A line does not in reality exist to mark the boundaries of an object against its surroundings or against other objects. Tone, colour, three-dimensional vision and movement tell us where the edges of objects are in real life.

The linear outline is a translation, an invented language, or rather the first phrases of a language with which we have learned to represent the visual world. Only higher primates seem to have the ability to read such statements, even domestic dogs and cats, living in homes where drawn images abound, seem to show no capability of recognizing other animals or themselves from outline drawings.

It is now so natural to accept an outline drawing as a depiction of reality, that it is sometimes thought of as the *only* way to draw, and that edges and perhaps sharp creases are the only features to be represented by these lines.

This is to forget that the outline *is* a series of invented marks which we humans have learned to interpret, and that therefore drawing in its most fundamental form is not a copying exercise as when a camera or a retina records, but an interpretation, and as such a great amount of different visual information can be depicted in many different ways as the language of visual expression evolves.

To return for a moment to our ancestors' cave drawings, it is interesting to note that the human figures which are on occasions depicted in company with the animals, usually attacking them, are treated quite differently, their shapes being interpreted as stick figures. It would

Detail from a wall painting in Tassili (Algeria).

Painted figures of running men. Left to right: Valltora Gorge (North Africa); Ghat (Fezzan); painting by Bushmen (South Africa).

seem that the precise outline of human figures was less interesting to early man, so stylized symbols sufficed.

Ancient Egyptian artists revealed a much greater interest in human form, even depicting the tools carried to signify occupation and the insignia of rank.

The Greeks of the Golden Age worshipped physical beauty and idealized it in beautifully observed but un-lifelike drawings. Their most naturalistic and lifelike evocations of human form were achieved in sculpture however – little comparable drawing survives.

Festival scenes from the tomb of the priest of Amun at Thebes.

Black-figure amphora from the late sixth century BC. Metropolitan Museum of Art, New York. Rogers Fund, 1914.

After a long period, over 1,000 years, during which depictions of human figures degenerated into rather sparse and uninformed imagery, the growth of realism began in the thirteenth century with Italian painters such as Giotto and Duccio. As the Italian Renaissance unfolded, drawing from life developed as never before until in the late fifteenth and early sixteenth century drawings by Raphael, Michelangelo and Leonardo da Vinci set new standards of observation, fluency and power.

These masters, drawing with pen and ink, chalk, charcoal and silverpoint on paper or prepared surfaces, were trying to extract from their models the information required for their paintings. While still depending on a linear outline they used it in conjunction with vigorous linear hatching and cross-hatching to suggest form and movement. Human anatomy was studied in detail and well understood. Michelangelo especially used the interplay of surface musculature to enhance the expressiveness of dramatic postures. As a result, perhaps not intentionally, the drawings had a validity and life of their own, quite separate from their function as studies for larger works.

At the same time in Germany Albrecht Dürer was exploring the possibilities of line-created tone and form in engravings and etchings in a style that was richly decorated. One hundred years later Rembrandt was using pen and ink line to express in a few shrewd strokes the fugitive effect of light on a group of figures.

In the next century Goya in Spain was taking the expressivity of line and tone to its extremes in his etchings of the Horrors of War.

Watteau, Boucher and Delacroix in France successively lightened the touch with witty and brilliant studies in pencil, chalk and wash. Ingres in the early nineteenth century had returned to classical imagery produced after the most intensively observed and painstakingly rendered studies. Only a little later, Auguste Rodin the French sculptor, expressed what *he* needed from the human form with the most spontaneous outline shapes filled in with quick washes. Degas and Schiele near the turn of the last century were exploring different aspects of the un-idealized appearance of real people, Beardsley and Klimt used flat decoration to express their ideas, while the impressionist Seurat drew only light.

So many styles, so many approaches to figure drawing. How should the would-be figure draughtsman start? Is there any element common to all great drawings? Yes, I think there is.

All the best figure drawings try to make a visual statement about the observed object. They do not try to convey all the possible information, but try to tell the truth succinctly and clearly about a chosen aspect. Good drawings are selective and single minded.

The following sequence of exercises is intended to help the beginner to draw objectively from the human figure using

Drawing of Haman by Michelangelo. British Museum, London.

this necessity to be selective as the guiding principle.

If used as a course, pursued with tenacity and enthusiasm, it should give a totally inexperienced and relatively inept beginner at least the ability to draw with understanding and honesty.

For those with some natural talent for whom the figure does not present so formidable a problem, I hope that following this ordered sequence will help to clarify aims and concentrate attention on enquiry and discovery.

It is absolutely vital to understand that drawing anything well requires more than technique. It is much more important to be honest and self critical, treating each drawing as a genuine search for greater knowledge. Curiously enough, setting out to draw a truthful rather than a beautiful drawing will often result in one that is truthful *and* beautiful. Some of the world's best drawings were made by artists who did not possess natural facility.

For me, and I am sure for most others who like me have been drawing all their lives, the excitement and challenge of drawing never diminishes. There is always something more to learn, some simpler more direct way to express things seen or experienced.

Good draughtsmanship is not acquired quickly or easily; there are no real short cuts. Tackling all the projects in this book may seem a daunting prospect, but taken one at a time and not looking too far ahead, I hope that the progressive discoveries you can make will carry you enthusiastically from project to project.

On the other hand, I would not want you to consider the order of the projects to be sacrosanct. Perhaps a project may spark off further ideas, or the type or availability of models and locations may make it difficult to comply exactly with the instructions. The sequence of projects may eventually be treated as a general outline only, or as something to fall back on if other ideas falter. It is also to be expected that some projects will need to be repeated, either because the objective has not been reached or perhaps because it *did* go well and pointed the way to further exploration on the same lines. All this is fine: the book is to be *used*; it does not provide all the answers. The answers are only to be found through the actual activity of drawing.

Perhaps some diffidence may be felt by a beginner asked to draw complete figures in the first session. I feel strongly that this method is preferable to the teaching sequence in which block drawings, simple diagrams of masses, anatomy and similar disciplines have to be mastered before progressing to real human beings.

It is much less dreary to plunge in boldly, draw what is seen with as few preconceptions as possible, learning the niceties and difficulties to be dealt with later as they are encountered.

Melancolia I (copperplate engraving) by Durer.
Kupferstichkabinett, Berlin.

Shape

In this section the emphasis will be upon learning how to see and draw the overall shape of the figure, simply and directly, with no attention to detail. The objective is to introduce an abstract view of the human figure to help clear away the many preconceptions which will have been built up in the mind, and which obscure accurate observation.

A fundamental requirement in drawing is the ability to see the real shape of an object without subjective distortion. I will try to explain what I mean by the term 'subjective distortion'.

In normal everyday life we have to react quickly and intuitively to our surroundings in order to move about and perform actions with safety and certainty. To achieve this our brain selects from the mass of visual information supplied by the eye, only those aspects which are useful in recognizing objects, judging distances, speeds of movement etc. A very important part of this interpretation is the ability of the brain to deduce from one view of an object, not only what it is, but what it would look like from another view, and it nearly always converts an unusual view into a

Fig.1

normal one, so that it can be recognized by matching with its stored memory image. For example the remembered image of say a wine bottle will always be an upright, longish form. But a bottle in life may be observed from above (fig.1), so that perhaps only a very small amount of its length can be seen. In this circumstance the bottle may actually present a shape to the eye which is very near to being circular, but in most cases the brain has no difficulty in interpreting the object and making a fair estimate of what its length and its shape would be if it was returned to the more familiar eye-level position. It does this by reference to the perspective distortion of the surroundings of the bottle, by reference to the usual length and appearance of other bottles, by comparing the slightly different views which the left eye and right eyes give (depth vision) and other subtle clues. It is very complicated and yet we do it instantly and are doing it all the time. Our judgment of whether to cross a road in front of a car depends on being able to judge the real distance of the vehicle and the real width of the road and from this and other facts the likelihood of reaching the other side safely. You do this time and time again, usually accurately, despite the fact that your eye records the *width* of the road as rather smaller than it does the same length applied across your vision.

Consider fig.2. Although dimension (a) representing the height of the building is much larger than dimension (b) representing the width of the road, the various perspective clues would lead your brain to deduce the *actual* width of the road that has to be crossed as perhaps as much as or more than the height of the building.

Now the important fact for you as an objective draughtsman is that it is the unprocessed, observed dimensions (a) and (b) that most concern you, not as in life, the calculated 'real' distance.

It may seem that I am dwelling unduly on this aspect but it really is at the root of *the* most common difficulty encountered in drawing by beginners. When attempting to draw the road and building, the brain tries to process what the eye sees so that the dimension (b) is stretched and drawn to occupy more depth in the picture despite its observed depth, because the brain knows that it is in reality a longer distance than it appears. But you must learn to ignore the interpretations of your subconscious brain and draw what your eye sees. It is hard to do this; the brain does not give up easily and is constantly processing your vision and catching you out. Luckily there are many ways of combatting this and helping your eye to see in the special direct way that it must in order to draw objectively.

One way is to train yourself to look for the overall flat shape occupied by an object, rather than assessing its height and width separately. If an object or part of an object can be loosely contained by a square or a circle, even if it does not fit precisely, it is very useful to imagine or even draw the square or circle around it. Triangles, rectangles, ovals, and irregular shapes close to these, are all easier to

judge relatively one to the other by eye than are linear dimensions.

The human form of course is *not* square, or any geometrical shape; it is its own shape or rather its own multitude of shapes depending on pose and viewpoint, but in many circumstances it is very useful to see it *contained* by one or other of these abstractions.

For projects 1 to 5 I suggest that soft pencil, chalk or, best of all, charcoal should be used for speed and simplicity.

Fig.2

Shape

Project 1

For the first project, very quick, very simplified but complete drawings are to be attempted.

The purpose is to develop your ability to see the whole shape of the figure in almost one glance and also, right from the start, to rid you of the preconceptions of the figure as a torso with long appendages. We all know it *is* that, but in order to draw well, relating the parts properly to the whole, you must try to empty your mind of preconceptions and see what it is in front of you as though it is entirely new. Arms and legs, when entwined with and enclosed by the torso, are as one form.

Ask your model to adopt a series of curled up poses, wrapping arms, legs, head and neck as far as possible into one combined form, as though sculpted from a square block. Start with poses held for ten minutes at first, then five.

Look at the complete pose and try to decide if most of it would fit into a square, a rectangle, a circle or some other regular geometrical shape.

If it does more or less fit one of these shapes, either draw the geometric shape and then the figure contained within it, or draw the figure contained by the shape in your mind's eye. Ignore details – forget the fact that entwined or hidden arms and legs can in other circumstances unravel and separate; draw what you see as one lumpy form. It can be a simple outline or a silhouette, but it must include the whole figure. It is better to draw an almost abstract shape which suggests the general shape of the pose than to complete only an arm, hand or head, no matter how beautifully it is drawn. To do this is to miss the point of the exercise.

Fig.1

Fig.2

Fig.3

13

Shape

Project 2

Any pose from project 1 is to be studied a little more carefully and drawn from several viewpoints. This is to show how the appearance of a form changes from different angles and eye levels.

As before, you should attempt very simple drawings of very short duration. Each time that you move your viewpoint, you will bring to the drawing something you have learnt from the previous one and hopefully you will progress towards a very full understanding of the principal forms and directions in the pose.

In order to decide on the overall shape of a pose it is sometimes helpful to cut a square hole in a piece of paper, view through the aperture and move it until it contains the pose as closely as possible. If it more or less fits the square,

Fig.1

Fig.2

there you have it. If it doesn't, note how much
of the square it does fill. It may be mostly in a
triangular half or a vertical or horizontal
rectangular half. Other quite subtle rectangular
proportions which are not so immediately
apparent without, can be easily appreciated
by viewing through this square view-finder.

At this stage, not only should you be assessing
the overall shape of the pose but also the
directions of the main planes which suggest
volume, the solid form of an object. A plane
can best be visualized as the direction in space
that a flat card would have if laid against the
model in such a way as to touch as much of the
surface or surfaces as possible. Sometimes the
imaginary card will fit very closely, as that
delineated on the lower back of the model in
fig.1. At other times it will only touch the
tops of several rounded forms but will
represent the *general* direction of the group.

Shape

Project 3

Ask the model to take up a simple, sitting or semi-reclining pose on the floor. Aim for something fairly compact, not so curled up as before perhaps, but keeping arms and legs quite closely into the main form. The purpose is to appreciate the figure as a form arising from and defining the ground plane.

Having seen how the complete figure can be thought of as occupying a flat geometric shape and then a three dimensional block, I would like you to think of the block sitting on the floor or ground plane.

The live model, in every situation where studied drawing is possible (i.e. not flying, falling or floating), will be in contact with the floor, either directly or indirectly. It is vitally necessary to consider all the planes of the figure relative to this 'ground plane'. Only by

cultivating an acute awareness of the positions of a figure with reference to the plane of the floor can the structure and balance of the figure supporting itself against the downward pull of gravity be properly understood and analysed.

Described in words, this concept sounds more complex than it is in reality. It is really only necessary to divert attention to the way in which the figure is, so to speak, erected on the ground plane, for it to be clearly seen and appreciated. However, it is not always so easy to *define* the ground plane by drawing. A regular grid pattern on the floor, as tiles or carpet squares, is very helpful in this respect.

Fig.1

16

Fig.2

Fig.4

Fig.3

Better still perhaps at this stage, is to place the model on a large square of paper or card, the perspective of which will clearly define the floor plane. Draw this square as part of the pose, paying as much attention to its shape and apparent plane as to the planes of the figure. Still try to ignore details, try above all to describe the general blocks and the angles made with the ground plane.

17

Shape

Project 4

Probably the most commonly adopted pose in life drawing is that of the seated model. For this reason it is sometimes felt to be rather boring but if some thought is given to the nature of the event when the human figure achieves equilibrium by close association with a series of struts and supports called a chair, there is really no necessity for boredom!

The model should initially be asked to sit on a chair in a simple posture, well and firmly located, feet flat on the floor and not too far from the legs of the chair, bottom well back into the angle between seat and chair back.

A space visitor, unfamiliar with either chairs or humans, would have no reason to suppose that this composite object could be separated into two parts, the animate part moving away from the inanimate support.

You should try to see the object in the same way. Draw the six-legged object as a complete structure arising from the ground plane even higher than the structures in the previous project.

Although there may be quite a lot of space between the chair seat and the floor, the legs of the chair are just as securely supporting the

Fig. 1

18

Fig.2

'building' as if they were walls rising from the base which is represented by the floor contained between the four corner supports.

Draw the planes which represent these walls and any others which simplify and generalize the total form. Try to see the rough shape a sculptor would have to have cut from an original cube of stone before he started to differentiate the specific figure and chair details.

Once this relationship between figure and chair has been seen and appreciated in a simple form, it can be seen in all the permutations of chair and figure and will remain a part of your vision of every seated figure.

Fig.3

19

Shape

Project 5

For this exercise the erection of the figure from the ground plane is completed: we have the standing figure.

Now before preconceptions about the human figure intervene, I want you to hold in your mind that idea of the standing figure as the thinnest shape you have yet considered in these exercises, but still a peg, a monolith, staying balanced upright because its base is at right angles to its centre line.

Of course, the actual ground contact area of a standing human figure is limited to the soles of the feet, but the weight of overhanging larger forms higher up is distributed so that gravity pulls equally all round and balance is maintained.

If you imagine strings falling vertically from the widest points all around a standing figure, you will have a sort of three-dimensional diagram of the forces which must be balanced (see fig.1).

The shape delineated on the floor represents its cast shadow if it were lit directly from above, and each pose will have a characteristic 'shadow', its shape and the position of the foot-contact areas within it representing its own particular diagram of forces.

Draw this diagram from observation of your

Fig.1

Fig.2

Fig.3

Fig.4

model's standing pose from several angles and distances.

You will find that it is easier to see both the 90-degree angle that the figure makes with the ground and the 'shadow' more clearly when the viewpoint is either rather raised or close to the model.

Another advantage of this is that the outline shape seen from close proximity or from any but an eye-to-eye level is unfamiliar and unexpected, which makes it less likely that you will draw what you think you know rather than what you see.

Look at fig.4. Objective observation of this standing figure tells us, for example, that the hands appear to be very close to the toes of the right foot. There is, of course, considerable *spatial* distance between them: we know this to be true because no human beings have arms which hang down to their feet – but this is a stumbling block – it is *because* we know this elementary fact that we tend to modify what we see to fall in with what we know.

Fig.3, shows diagrammatically how parts of an object which are situated on a line of sight will appear together two dimensionally although there may be considerable actual three-dimensional space between them. From the longer viewpoint A, the hands will be seen to rest in the 'normal' expected place i.e. fingertips about half way down the thigh. Approach to position B though, and the lines of sight bring hands and forward foot into close confluence, and widen the distance between the feet, which are now viewed from almost directly above.

The whole secret of foreshortening is contained in this concept.

Heads, hands and feet

Having used twelve pages of drawings and text to urge you to observe and draw the figure as one simple entity, it may seem rather retrogressive of me to suggest that the head, hands and feet should now be singled out for special attention.

I *do* feel that it is generally rather dangerous to make lots of unrelated studies of small sections of the body, especially separate facial features. I consider that too much of this fragmented drawing makes it more difficult when you come to draw the complete figure to see its essential unity.

The complete head however, and to a lesser extent, the hands and feet, are rather exceptional and often present special difficulties for the beginner.

Part of the trouble lies in the comparative complexity of these forms, but much more fundamental is the difficulty of seeing them clearly and objectively. In everyday life we are continually reacting to visual messages from the facial features of other people, with or without the support of speech. We are capable of

Fig. 1

Fig.2

Fig.3

detecting very subtle changes in the shape of eyes and mouth and surrounding areas which interact with these features, and we can and do deduce a great variety of information by reading the signs.

We should know what such a familiar thing as the human head looks like. Unfortunately it is precisely the fact that we think we *do* know what it looks like that prevents us from looking at it objectively. We are so used to reading signals from especially expressive areas of the face and unconsciously rejecting comparatively blank areas that it carries over into our observation of the head when we want to make a drawing, with the result that the *same* interesting bits monopolise our attention.

The result is a sort of symbol of a head in which the facial area looms large and the eyes, nose and mouth occupy an inordinately large area within that.

To draw the head as it is, we have to combat this 'processing' of the picture received by our eyes, and learn to consider the less expressive areas *between* the features and to give the facial area its proper size and shape relative to the whole head.

Curiously enough we already have an acutely sensitive appreciation of the interrelated areas of the head and face, which we use in recognition of individuals, but it is so subliminal that most people find it impossible to extract these stored patterns in order to draw them. To check this, try drawing from memory the complete head of someone that you have never drawn from life, but whose face you know very well. If you produce a good convincing likeness you have a very unusual visual memory.

This problem of familiarity gets in the way of objective vision, and contributes to the difficulty that most people encounter when drawing hands and feet too, but to a lesser extent.

The following projects are designed to help you to see these 'familiar' areas with a more direct and objective eye.

23

Heads, hands and feet

Fig.1

Project 1

Pose your model in any comfortable reclined pose, with head and face resting horizontal to your vision.

Unless you tilt *your* head to get a 'normal' upright view of the model's face, you will now have in view a form in which the two eyes are one *above* the other, the ridge of the nose lies horizontally and all together it is fairly unfamiliar.

Observe and draw it from this angle, resisting the temptation to tilt your head for the normal view. Treat the shapes and volumes as though they were completely new and unfamiliar forms. Look for general linking planes as in the Shape projects.

It may be as well to draw the neck and

shoulders or even more of the figure as well. The point of this exercise is to view the head and face from an unfamiliar angle, so as long as that is complied with, there is no reason why the figure should not be completed.

Later try drawing a pose where you have a completely upside-down view of the face as in my drawings. The heads of these figures were drawn totally without turning the drawing board round to check that it looked right the

other way up, but after completion a 'normal' upright view of the drawn head revealed that a good likeness had been achieved, which perhaps proves something!

Although my drawings here are in pencil, I suggest that you may find it easier initially to generalize and simplify the forms using charcoal, but it is not important and if you find you need the greater precision of pencil, that's fine.

Fig.2

Fig.3

Heads, hands and feet

Project 2

For this session a series of poses should be set up involving head, hands and feet in a variety of close associations as suggested by the drawings on this spread.

Hands are capable of many actions but they are especially good at gripping, when they wrap around objects and in a sense take on the shape of the object that they enwrap. If you draw them like this, not only can you use them to help describe the enfolded form, but you can also illuminate their own shape by studying the form that they are holding.

It all helps to keep you looking at composite forms and not getting tied up with surface detail. Fingers can be spread of course and so can toes, but fingers most often combine with the palm to make simple shapes, even a relaxed hand is cupped in shape.

The palm of the hand is often represented as a flat squarish rigid form to which the fingers are attached, but it is not like this at all. It moves *with* the fingers and thumb and should be seen as a form continuous with them, arching when the fingers are stretched and spread, and cupping when they curl.

Feet are much less mobile, but still plagued by preconception-engendered difficulties. They have splendidly strong arched structures which make the under surface concave, so that the middle to inner border of the sole does not touch the ground in the normal standing position. The area that *does* contact the ground however is pressed by the weight of the body to the shape of the ground plane, usually in the studio a flat surface.

You must try to visualize this flattened surface in the supporting foot and make it fit the plane with which you represent the ground.

Fig.1

Fig.2

Fig.3

Heads, hands and feet

Project 3

Have the model sit comfortably in good light
to give strong modelling to the face and head.
A cross light from one side is usually good.
If the source is too far behind the head, you
will need a light surface to reflect some light
back into the shadows of the face.

Having hopefully rid yourself of some of
what you think you know about the head and
face, this project is to allow you to re-look at
the 'normal' view and try to see it anew.

One of the hardest things to get right is the
proportion of facial area to the rest of the head.
This varies from individual to individual, but
it usually comes as rather a surprise, when
measured, to see how little of the total head
area is taken up by the eyes, nose and mouth
features.

The skull gives the shape to the head and
face. It is unique in the body in having a
complete bony structure near the surface. Most

Fig.2

of the cranium is covered by a very thin
muscular sheet and the main modification of
the facial form of the skull is made by the
inclusion of the eyes in their orbits and the
extension of the small bony ridge of the nose
by cartilage into the familiar nose shape. The
only muscles with any bulk are those which
activate the jaw bone, the masseters, and even
these to a great extent are underlying the angle
of the jaw, having no visible effect on the
surface form.

It follows that to understand the skull is to
understand the basic forms of the head and
face, so if it is possible to have access to a good
plastic skull, it is worth making some drawings
of it from a variety of angles, paying particular
attention to the proportions and directions of
its main planes.

Failing this, study drawings of skulls and
try to recognize the same forms beneath the
skin of the live model.

Fig.2 in the introduction to this section shows
a skull with the top of the cranium removed.
The shape of the section so revealed shows that
the side planes are fairly flat and that they are
not parallel, but converge a little towards the
brow, the widest part of the head being much

Fig.1

Fig.3

Fig.4

nearer to the back. It can be seen also that the plane of the forehead (at right angles to the skull centre line) is repeated by the front parts of the cheekbones (zygomatic arches). Note the semi-circular arc of the mouth and teeth, a form which in life dictates the direction of the lips.

Concentrate on those forms and try to draw them before you draw the more obvious eyes, nose and mouth features. I don't mean that you should ignore these features; the angle made by a line joining the eyes tells you a lot about the angle of the front plane of the face, the angle of the mouth does too, and the side planes of the nose have to be placed so that they rise at equal angles to the face plane. But it is their *positions* that you have to establish, and the area that you think they occupy together, not their individual shapes, not yet, that comes later.

It is helpful in deciding how the features are placed, to think of the centres of the eyes as being the points of the base of an inverted triangle, the apex being in the middle of the mouth. The shape of this triangle, and its size relative to the rest of the face, can be initially judged and is a very important shape to get right.

When the pattern of the face is right, it will already look a little or a lot like the sitter; delineating the detailed feature characteristics is just dotting the 'i's and crossing the 't's.

Weight

In this section we give consideration to the weight of the figure and try to see how its forms react to the constant pull of gravity.

Projects from the first section (Shape) explored forms gradually building from the ground up, so to speak. Now we should look rather at the forces which try to pull them back down again.

Bodies come in all shapes and sizes, but all are composed of comparatively soft tissue, which is prevented from becoming a heap by clinging to a system of hard supports called the skeleton. Some of the soft tissue is purely suspended, the viscera, fat, genitals etc., and some contributes to the stiffness of the skeleton and operates it, muscles, tendons, cartilage etc. More will be said of the bones and muscular systems under the Anatomy heading, but for the moment it is enough to observe which forms seem to resist gravity and those which bend and sag.

Overweight subjects will reveal the omnipresent force more obviously than will very thin models, and the decision to concentrate attention in a drawing on this aspect may well be prompted by the over-powering 'weightiness' of a well-upholstered model, which is a fine and good reason for drawing it so.

But my intention in these next exercises is to draw attention to the way *all* figures are affected by gravity when they are at rest.

The figure in movement, while still being

Fig.1

subject to the force of gravity, is generating forces and movements of its own, which can be added to the gravitational pull in some places, while subtracting from or multiplying it in others. A leaping figure, for example, immediately before take off from one leg may have transferred all body weight to that leg, which will be tensed and taut under the strain, while the other leg is being thrown upward and outward, its tissues apparently defying gravity.

At rest, on the other hand, the pull on the body is all one way and it is arrested either by contact with the ground or by the limit of its suspension.

It is the way that it adapts itself to the constant pull, the way that, depending on the ground plane, it tells us where that plane is that must be the primary interest. It is this that will enable us to make a drawing that expresses the subjective feeling of mass and weight.

Fig.2

Weight

Project 1

Set the pose with the model seated simply on a chair, legs together, arms by side, feet firmly on the floor, back against the chairback. Draw figure and chair as one as before, the chair legs taking over from the human legs as main supports of the weight of the body. Gravity works inexorably on all forms without distinction; those forms that can give to that pull, will do so. Try to see the tissues being tugged earthwards by this invisible force.

At half time tip the pose through ninety degrees, so that the model is on her back, but arranged on the chair as though sitting. Try to recreate the earlier pose as accurately as possible and do a second drawing preferably on the same piece of paper, and from a viewpoint which gives the same or similar perspective. Look carefully at the changes in the forms – they are the same features but the switch in direction of gravity relative to the figure changes them into something quite different.

It is very interesting to view the resultant drawings in the wrong context, i.e. the reclined pose as an upright seated pose and vice versa. Of the two drawings on these pages only the left-hand drawing has been printed the right way up, as indicated by the downward direction of gravity.

Fig. 1

Notice how the soft tissues of the breasts and stomach tend to be pulled downwards along the torso in fig.1 and *across* the torso in the new downward direction in the other drawing. Also, less obviously, in the lying figure the base of the rib cage is left high, the shoulders pulled down and the neck is at a completely different angle in response to the weight of the head.

In short, the main weight of the seated figure is supported on the base of the pelvis, while in the lying figure support is distributed along the length of the back. Gravity acts on facial tissues in the same way, which is one reason why the head should be drawn in the position that you see it, without turning your own head to see the model's face the 'right' way up.

On this page the figure looks wrong, almost like a figure pinned to a wall of death by centrifugal force, but if the book is rotated through 90 degrees so that the gravity arrow points downward, all will be well, and the other drawing will look wrong.

If your drawings *don't* look wrong when viewed the 'wrong' way, you have missed the pull of gravity.

Fig.2

Weight

Project 2

On as hard a surface as your model is prepared to tolerate, set a relaxed reclining pose something like the ones on these pages.

Since the human figure does not have regular side and front planes as a regular geometric architectural block has, it cannot be lain on its side to rest unmodified on a flat plane. In these circumstances it must perforce adapt its shape to the rigid surface as best it can.

As we have seen, gravity tugs continuously at soft and rigid forms alike, but they react rather differently to its influence.

A fully reclined figure initially achieves much more comprehensive contact with the ground plane than does the standing figure, and the action of gravity increases this contact area.

As shoulder and hip are rigidly supported by their bony structures, the major adaptation to the flat surface is made by the sling-like lateral curvature of the back bone, cancelling out the hollow of the waist on the contact side, and greatly exaggerating the curves on the upper side.

Look carefully again for all the outward visible signs of the force of gravity at work. Set yourself the task of expressing just this aspect of the pose above all others.

Try to imagine the shape of the part of the body that has been flattened into contact with the ground. Try placing large sheets of paper or board under the model and drawing a line closely round the contact areas. When the model moves away, the 'imprint' shape is very revealing and interesting. It can be copied while the model is resting and incorporated into your drawing.

In both the very similar poses drawn here, the model has made the hip area more comfortable and balanced by rotating the pelvis a little to distribute weight along the lower thigh. As a result the abdomen (and its quite heavy contents) is tipped forwards to be pulled towards the floor by its own weight. The amoung of sag varies, of course, with the elasticity of the individual model's muscle tone, but some effect is always visible. Breasts too change shape in this position. Note how in fig.1

Fig.1

the nearer breast is pulled by gravity away from the chest wall, while her left breast is spread and flattened by its contact with the ground.

Main limbs, with their rigid long bones, cannot bend but must pivot under gravity to achieve a position of rest or else be used as props to support other forms.

Again, in the drawings on this page, see how the legs have adapted their own weight to the ground surface, while one arm is supporting the head, transmitting its weight to the elbow and distributing it along the upper arm.

Fig.2

Weight

Project 3

This time pose the model on a soft surface that will 'give' to the weight of the reclined or semi-reclined figure. A softly sprung settee or soft mattress is ideal.

Although I have not repeated the poses exactly here, you could do so and then make direct comparisons with the rigid support for the figure in the last project.

On this soft support the hard projections of the figure can make hollows to accommodate themselves and extremes of pelvic swing are not necessary.

Soft tissues are still pulled downwards but where before they made contact with the rigid plane of the floor and were compelled to spread out and flatten, now they bury themselves. Sometimes their line of contact with the soft support is depressed out of sight, so cutting off your view of part of the figure and apparently narrowing it.

It is most important, when this occurs, to understand what is happening and to draw the emergence of the soft support *in front* of the obscured part of the figure so that it is very clear that the rest of the figure *is* there, but sunk out of sight by its own weight.

A combination of soft and hard supports for the figure can be interesting too. In fig.2 all the weight of the model is taken by the settee and transmitted to the floor by its four legs, except for the model's left leg which emerges from the hollow made by the torso, depressing

Fig.1

Fig.2

the edge of the settee with its partial weight and supporting the rest by the light contact of foot on floor.

Note that it is still possible to use props: even a soft support only gives so far. The model's near arm is propping up her shoulder in this instance and gently arresting the tendency of gravity gradually to slide her head and shoulders deeper into the angle of the sofa.

Rather more light and shade has crept into this drawing than was strictly necessary to express the idea of softly supported weight, but the light was interesting too and it's not always easy to be totally single minded!

Fig.3

Weight

Project 4

In this project the pose has been set up to involve several supports and props allowing the weight of the body to be widely distributed.

In a semi-reclined position much of the body weight is supported between the pelvis and the shoulder girdle. Hence the model's torso is 'slung' between the support of her firmly lodged right upper arm and her tipped pelvis. The right arm also functions as a prop for the head. Her right leg has been allowed to fall and is in contact with the ground along all its length, in contrast to the other leg in which the weight is balanced and transferred to the firmly planted foot. Neither leg is supporting anything but itself and the far arm is hanging slackly. These are the movements to sort out and express here, and there are many clues.

Note the rounded shape of the model's right breast pulled up by the propped and propping arm contrasting with the slacker form of the breast on the relaxed side. Also the swing of the torso in this position allows the weight of the viscera to round out the lower side while leaving the hard edge of the pelvic girdle visible on the upper side. There is also a flatness to the edge of the weight-taking foot, the whole length of her right lower leg and what can be seen of the model's left buttock – all these forms are flattened by gravity in contrast with a hard base surface.

Incidentally the left hand figure below was drawn *after* the more studied version, in an attempt to express the relaxed weight of the torso more clearly. It often happens that the essential movement becomes clearer as one drawing is completed, either because one's understanding of the pose has become less cluttered or perhaps that the model has relaxed more into the pose. So in either case it is quite reasonable to add a quick statement of the newly seen movement to the original drawing.

Fig.1

Fig.2

Fig.3

Balance

Having learned something about the way that the pull of gravity is made evident in the seated and reclining figure, I now suggest that you pursue the subject of weight distribution by considering the balancing acts performed by human figures when standing upright.

Objects with weight close to the ground and broad bases have no problem maintaining equilibrium.

As objects become taller and relatively smaller based, equilibrium becomes increasingly precarious, until eventually the slightest inequality of the downward pull of gravity, or deviation of the direction of pull from 90 degrees to the base, results in the object falling over.

In this context we have to refer to a vertical line through the centre of a figure about which weight must be distributed equally if the figure is to maintain its balance. We can call this the centre line of gravity.

It is a very useful concept in drawing the figure, as the head of an upright standing pose is nearly always balanced at the top of this imaginary vertical, the centre of weight being directly below it.

Where weight is distributed equally between the feet, as in the soldier's position of attention, the vertical line will descend from the head to a point between the heels, and the same will apply in any position of equal weight between wider spaced feet; the centre of gravity will be directly above a point midway between the weight-taking heels. I say heels, rather than feet, because most of the weight of the body in an erect but relaxed pose is transmitted to the ground via the heels – the rest of the foot is mainly functioning to maintain balance.

If the weight of the figure is mainly supported by one leg, as is the case more often than not, then the weight-taking heel will be seen to be

Fig.1   on or near this vertical line from the base of

40

the cranium. Supporting the weight of the body in this way on one leg implies taking the weight *off* the other one, and the relaxed result of this is that the hip on the side unsupported by the non-weight-taking leg, drops to an angle where the base of the spine is supporting itself with the minimum of muscular activity. In this situation the upper part of the body would be thrown to one side of the centre line of gravity and would fall unless some counter balance was made. This is achieved by a counter swing of the upper body so that at the shoulders a

tilt contrary to the hip tilt is maintained at exactly the right angle to bring the head back to its position vertically above the main ground contact.

It should be said that this rule is not absolutely precise or infallible, but drawing a vertical line and observing carefully how the shapes and volumes of your standing figure distribute themselves relative to it is fascinating and informative.

For example, movements of the arms subtly affect the distribution of weight about the centre line. If the arms are actually contributing to the support of the body at all, as in fig.1 where the model's lean is arrested some way from the vertical by the arms, the head is clearly seen to be well to the right of a vertical through the feet i.e. the figure is in a sort of arrested equilibrium; if the grip of the hands was released, she would immediately fall backwards.

In the figure on this page (fig.2), however, the model's left arm is only really supporting itself on the easel, very little of any body weight being transferred through it, and what little weight is lost there to the equation is balanced by the akimbo right arm.

Balance is fundamental to the understanding of the standing figure and absolutely essential in drawing.

Fig.2

41

Balance

Project 1

Set a standing pose to throw as much body weight on to one leg as possible, and by separating the feet by at least 8 or 9 inches promote a strong tilt of the pelvis. You should aim for plenty of movement and counter balance in the pose, consistent with the model being as relaxed as possible.

Standing poses, especially if they are free-standing and unsupported, are hard to maintain, and you should mark the feet positions on the floor as soon as the pose is set, and tell your model to shift the bodyweight to the other leg from time to time as it gets painful and to stop posing at the faintest sign of the onset of giddiness. In any case it is probably necessary to rest a standing pose every half hour, although some experienced models maintain hour long poses without difficulty.

When drawing, search diligently for that centre of gravity line, then try to place the centre line of the weight-taking leg at the correct angle to it. If a reasonable degree of pelvic swing has been adopted by the model, the angle of the locked supporting leg will not be vertical and the hip on that side will jut out considerably. Do not *underplay* this move-ment: it is better to overdo it.

Note the positions of the feet, not just relative to each leg, but relative to each other. Try to see the pattern that the contact surfaces of the feet make and what shape on the floor would contain them.

Look for the counterswing of the upper body. Check the centre line of the torso against imaginary verticals if it is a front view, use the line of the spine in a back view.

Look for shoulder-tilt-angle compensating for hip swing; lines linking left and right hip bones, shoulder blades, collar bones are helpful in this respect; see Anatomy section for more details about these and other useful landmarks.

Above all, question your drawing at all stages.

Put down marks to denote the main movements, add secondary shapes based on them and check the emerging pattern of shape. If it doesn't quite ring true, suspect the first

Fig.1

lines; maybe you are building on a false premise – drawing is a process of searching and change. If after two hours' drawing you see something fundamentally wrong, to change which would ruin some beautifully finished bits of drawing on which you have laboured long, don't hesitate, change it.

One statement which says something forceful about the whole pose, is much more worth-while than any number of uncoordinated pieces of descriptive detail, however pretty.

Fig.2

Fig.3

43

Fig.1

Balance

Project 2

In this session the aim will be to produce drawings, either side by side or even, by using contrasting colours of line, superimposed on each other.

The pose should initially be a totally symmetrical standing position with the feet firmly placed about 12 inches apart, arms hanging free.

First try to discover what point on the ground is vertically below the centre of the head.

Masters of drawing from the earliest days have needed a plumb line to assist them in determining these vertical links and it is still a good idea, at least until you have developed a keen inner sense of the vertical. Any small but reasonably weighty object suspended by string or cotton between your eye and the model will serve to determine not only the line of centre of gravity, but also many other vertical correlations lining up with known vertical features in the studio can be a great help too.

Fig.2

As in all the exercises, but in this one especially, move around the pose before you start, and be prepared during the making of your drawing to leave your position and look again from other viewpoints.

Thus while drawing a standing figure from a front view, you may be unsure whether points which lie on the same vertical plumb line from *this* view, are indeed truly above each other in depth. A plumb line check from the side view will tell you the answer immediately, and enable you better to understand and draw the solid geometry from the front.

Having analysed the symmetrically balanced pose, ask your model to move, without significantly changing the feet placement on the floor, so that the body weight is taken up by one leg more than the other. Make sure

that this new pose is really relaxed and stable.

Now look and compare what you see with your first drawing. Try to discover the adjustments that the body has made to adapt to the asymmetric support. Look especially for the distribution of body weight each side of a plumb line from the head, and how near to the weight taking foot is the point where this line meets the floor.

Then, try other variations on the theme: twisting, tilting, bending forwards with the arms propping the upper body, or backwards with the arms hanging free (very difficult to hold for more than a few moments).

Analyse and compare each pose, and judge your drawings only by their appearance of stability. If your figures look as though they may fall over, look again at the pose.

Fig. 3

Fig. 4

Fig. 5

45

Balance

Project 3

In setting up the pose for this exercise, what you should be looking for is a standing position which is receiving some help to maintain balance and so is rather more of a 'lean'.

To have sufficient time for a thorough analysis of the weight distribution the pose should not be too extreme, your model must be reasonably relaxed while supporting some body weight by suspension from, or propping against, a surface or an upright. The secondary support should be just enough for it to be clear that without it, the figure would fall over.

Analyse as before. Try to see the inclined weight being pulled over by gravity and prevented from falling by the prop of arm or shoulder.

The direction of lean need not necessarily be towards a support, but can be the other way as described and illustrated in the introduction to this section, where the model's backward lean is arrested by the extension of her arms from her light grip on the fixed upright. (In this case, the upright was a fixed ladder and was not vertical, hence the opposite lean in this drawing).

In these situations, the greater the degree of inclination of the figure from the vertical, the more tension there must be in the legs to maintain its rigidity, and the more compression or tension there must be in the supporting limbs.

Such considerations, however, are edging in to another area which will be investigated more fully in the Dynamics section. For the moment I suggest that you should concentrate on making sure that the imbalance of the standing figure but for its secondary support is made clear. Later on the pose can be referred to and considered again in the light of later discoveries about dynamics.

This is the whole point. Good poses can be returned to again and again. They are always a little different, very different with different models, and there is always another way to look at them, more to see and discover.

Fig.1

Fig.2

Fig.3

Structure

In this section the emphasis will be on more detailed analysis of the solidity of the human figure and how it holds together. Weight and balance, investigated in previous sections, are part of this, but the logic of structure ties these elements together.

Such a relatively complex form as the human figure with its numerous hollows, mobile limbs, hair appendages, local colour etc., can sometimes be seen more clearly as a wrapped package. It is then rather akin to the first rough stages of a stone carving, where basic directions of main planes are established before they are elaborated.

Drawing as a sculptor works, first finding the large forms and progressing in stages towards smaller and smaller detailed forms is a perfectly valid mode of working, but I intend it more as a way of looking and thinking about the structure of the figure.

The two photographs demonstrate this very clearly. Using two models juxtaposed, creates a composite form which is more abstract, less human, and therefore easily seen in terms of inanimate masses, or even of landscape. If it had been possible to coat the models in plaster of paris so as to eliminate details, it would have been ideal; but since this was clearly not practicable or humane we had to try to achieve the same effect by wrapping them in fabric. We tried as far as possible to eliminate folds and revelation of underlying detail by differential tensions in the cloth, trying only to simplify multiple forms into broad, simple ones.

Once one has seen these what I call 'averaged out' planes, it is quite easy to 'see' them still, even when the wrapping is removed.

It is not then necessary to draw these averaged planes explicitly, but just to let their presence in your mind's eye assist you to place the more complex forms accurately.

Remember, when searching for structure, the marks do not need to be pretty – any sort of dot, line, tick or smudge will do if it helps to explain what is going on. Such drawing should be thought of as explanation and analysis, not as description or imitation.

Fig.1

Fig.2

Fig.3

Fig.4

Structure

Project 1

Pose the model in a kneeling position, sitting back on the floor, perhaps splaying the feet, or with knees apart. This simulates a wide stable base, in architectural terms, surmounted by a sort of high-rise block. Such a position is fairly relaxed, the pelvis firmly seated, the support pillar of the spinal column held in balanced upright position by its guy ropes, the spinal muscles, and surmounted by the head.

Look for the triangular stability of this structure; think of it in an architectural way and try to express its internal structure rather than the external cladding. Charcoal is very good for this, as structure lines can be

Fig.2

Fig.1

50

Fig.3

committed to paper boldly and gradually lost as the cladding is added.

Ask the model to kneel up from the previous position. Now the architecture is less stable, more dependent on adequate bracing. The base is still large, the 'tower block' still upright, but its stability depends on the angle between the upper and lower leg being maintained strongly and correctly.

This angle, as would be expected, is normally a right angle, the lower legs lying on the ground plane, and the thighs vertical. Depending on the stance of the upper body the angle will change to achieve equilibrium, as will be seen by asking the model to raise both arms in front of her when the torso leans back slightly to balance the weight.

Fig.1 shows a wide triangular base ABC and 'tower block' of torso rising from the stable platform. Note the variations of the torso from the true vertical, and try to place the head in position relative to the vertical structure. Horizontal lines through the shoulders, nipples, pelvic girdle etc. can be seen as storeys in the vertical structure, subject to the same laws of perspective as a building would be.

In fig.2 I have boxed the vertical block, so as to clarify the way that the human torso swings and counterswings within it, and yet can be closely surrounded by such vertical scaffolding. As can be seen, the front of the thighs and lower stomach are flat against the front of the imaginary box, then the forms swing away until the shoulder blades touch the imaginary plane at the *back* of the box. The neck carries the swing back again, so that her chin is back to the front of the box again, forming the apex of a triangle of which the nipples form the base.

Fig.3. Rounding the forms to a more human idiom, the architecture can still be the motive for a drawing – even though the scaffolding is not explicit.

Structure

Project 2

Stand the model on a table and move your drawing board up close in order to get a low eye-level view.

If it is not possible to raise the model to table top height, a low eye level can be achieved, albeit less comfortably, by kneeling or lying on the floor close to the model and looking up.

From this view the figure has a monumental appearance. The feet, being on or near eye level, are seen near the same horizontal level but higher up the figure horizontal sections are apparently tipped away from your eye at ever increasing angles. It is essential to get these angles right, to be conscious of the way in which the forms of pelvis and thorax interlock.

This is very much the same as the last exercise but in reverse. The building is taller, with a smaller base and viewed from ground level, but the same rules apply. Wherever storeys can be defined by lines through twin elements like pelvic crests, nipples, shoulders, cheek bones etc. their angles should be determined with care.

Checking points on your by now, I hope, inbuilt mental grid will reveal interesting correlations which differ from more usual eye levels the further up the figure you look.

For example, note on fig.1 that the underside of the model's right breast (left hand in the drawing) is about on the same horizontal grid as the junction of upper and lower near arm, and that, further up, the chin is about on a level with the near shoulder. By contrast the knees are very much on the same level and the pelvis does not seem as tipped as would have been expected from such a low view. The reason for this is that the model is supporting most of her weight on her right leg and relaxing and bending her left leg, so allowing the pelvis to tip *against* and partly cancel out the apparent perspective angle.

You will find it interesting to introduce twists and other movements which you explored in the Weight section, and see how such poses are modified by the extreme eye level. The drawings 2 and 3 are two views of the same low eye-level pose in which, while the weight is fairly evenly distributed between the two legs, the upper part of the body is rotated relative to the pelvis, thereby introducing more variations of upward perspective.

Fig.1

Fig.2

Structure

Project 3

This time the interlocking forms of the figure are to be viewed from a high eye level which is not the easiest thing to arrange in every studio.

To be able to look down on a standing figure your drawing position must be raised by a few feet.

The vantage point for the drawing on this page (fig.3) was a gallery about eight feet above the floor. From this height there is considerable foreshortening of the figure and changes in the section can be easily seen. Such perspective is akin to the view of a skyscraper from a helicopter, while the perspective resulting from standing close to the model and looking down is more like the view of a skyscraper from the top windows of an adjoining block. In the former the floors (or sections) are arranged as fig.1 while in the latter they are more as fig.2.

Clear appreciation of the way that the sections change their angle to your eye and relate to the ground plane, is what you should be after in these exercises.

You should be searching for a strong piece of architecture which stands firmly on a discernable base, and which ascends from that base at right angles to it, so that your viewpoint is consistently verified by your drawing.

Everything must be subordinated to this end, line and tone used only to search for and describe the coherence of the structure, not to copy light and shade or surface texture and detail.

Many students' drawings begin strongly in the search for structure but degenerate into superficial copying in the later stages. It is difficult to maintain your analytical vision,

Fig.1   Fig.2

Fig.3

Fig.5

Fig.4

especially as the familiar areas of head, hands and feet are approached. It is relatively easy to see the planes and box structures of the torso, but facial features, fingers and toes tend to deflect attention from the basic planes of which they are only relatively superficial details. You must look past the familiar details and search for the basic form of even these smaller structures.

Breasts on the female model, in this context, need to be seen as they structurally are, as appendages attached to and supported by the thorax or rib cage. It is sometimes easier to link the plane of the front of the thorax above and below the breasts as though the breasts didn't exist, and to suspend them from that plane as you find its structural place. Once this relationship has been clearly seen and understood by drawing in this way, it may only be necessary in future to watch for the continuity of the thorax under the breasts while structuring breast and thorax together.

Fig.1

Structure

Project 4

Arrange the model in a simple lying pose. What
you should be looking for is a structure
reminiscent of a long, low building, or to
change the metaphor, a series of slopes, cliffs,
overhangs and plateaux. Poses lying on the
side as on this page, give good opportunities to
explore a variety of low-height structures.

I find it helpful to think oneself into the
situation where the foreground ground plane is
a beach, the figure representing the cliff.

In fig.1, you would assume that the flat
mattress was the beach, then as you approach
the small of the back you encounter a sudden
vertical cliff face. In fact it is more than
vertical, it is tipped back towards you, and
this backwards tilt becomes more extreme if
you move left. The approach opposite the
shoulder blade has a huge overhang, and I have
tried to understand and draw attention to these
angles by drawing little triangles which would
fit under the varying degrees of overhang.

If it had been possible to negotiate these
overhanging cliffs at, say, the waist area, the
summit attained would be a low ridge leading
away, round the higher ridge of the haunch and
then presumably to the descent.

Approaching from a point on the beach
further to the right presents a completely
different aspect. The rounded buttock form is
flattened by gravity, and after the initial,
mainly vertical face (with a foothold or two in
the cleft!), the slope becomes much less steep
and culminates in a wide-domed plateau, its
high point being the widest part of the model's
hip (great trochanter – see Anatomy section).

Other approaches, not necessarily at right
angles to the length of the figure, present a
different series of planes, all of which can be
appreciated the more vividly for the analogy
with topography.

As always, viewing the same structure from
other directions and heights, deepens your

understanding of the original viewpoint and
presents ncw problems and possibilities.

The other view of the pose here (fig.2) shows
how narrow is the low ridge at the waist,
giving way quickly to steeply undulating
downslopes. The way that the summit of the
hip gives way to the shallow downslope of the
upper thigh can be more clearly seen, but at the
same time the space under the overhang of the
back is not so obviously appreciated.

Fig.2

Structure

Project 5

A more complex reclining pose should be tried this time, employing a variety of supports, floor, raised surface and props.

Figure 4 shows what I mean. The support surface in this case was constructed with the use of some boxes and a folded mattress arranged to make varied levels and an inclined plane, all covered by a sheet.

Some, perhaps most of the weight of the torso is being supported by the pelvis, which in turn is supported by a lower part of the raised surface. The torso has relaxed sideways onto the inclined surface, the abdomen falling that way to leave the hip bone (iliac crest, see Anatomy section) prominent, and is also partially propped up by the right arm. Although unseen, it can be deduced that the right arm is propping to some extent by the attitude of the flopped-over head, the weight of which has to be supported.

Also propped is the model's right thigh, held horizontal by the lower leg and foot in contact with the floor. In contrast the other leg falls directly to the floor from the hip, to form what could be thought of as a long sloping ramp, as

opposed to the vertical face and plateau of the right leg.

It is probably a good place here to reconsider the problem of foreshortening.

In the introduction to Shape, I cited the example of a wine bottle seen from near to one end and therefore making a shape not far from circular, and yet being recognized as a shape which from a 'normal' viewpoint is long and cylindrical i.e. bottle shaped.

The low and high eye-level views in this section will have forced you to consider the foreshortened shapes of the torso, and in many of the other projects foreshortened views of limbs will have occurred. If you are still experiencing difficulty or are nervous when presented with foreshortened views, consider the diagram fig.2, which demonstrates how the apparent length of the arm diminishes from its actual length to no more than its actual width as it rotates to the most extreme position of pointing directly towards the eye of the observer. In this latter position the hand can be expected to appear bigger than the total space taken up by the complete arm.

Now try looking at your foreshortened arm in the mirror. Prop it so that you can take time to observe it at length and then draw what you see. Forget that it is an arm, which you know

Fig.1

to have greater length than width, and draw only the two-dimensional area that it covers in your view, on the picture plane, if you prefer.

You should come up with something rather like fig.3. More extremely foreshortened views of the torso than can easily be arranged in a standing pose, can be arrived at simply by observing a fully reclining pose from either end. In fig.1 I have searched for the way that the cross sections fit together, discovering such interesting correlations as for example the top of the model's shoulder being offset to the right from, or further *down* her body than, her left hip.

In this drawing, incidentally, the searching was made initially by the use of dots, lines of dots eventually being confirmed by a continuous line. This is a useful way to handle a completely ineradicable medium which only makes absolutely black marks.

Fig.4

Fig.5

Fig.2

Fig.3

59

Fig. 1

Anatomy

scapula spines

vertebral column (back bone)

olecranon (elbow)

olecranon (elbow)

posterior iliac spines

ulna

inner and outer malleolus

In the preceding sections I have made mention from time to time of certain anatomical features of the body which can be 'read' from the surface form and which help to sort out what is happening in a pose.

I have tried to keep to everyday terms such as hip, shoulder blade, spine etc., so that no special anatomical knowledge has been required in order to identify the features.

Theoretically, in order to draw the human figure, knowledge of what lies beneath the surface of the skin is not absolutely necessary. If observation of the surface is acute enough and the planes and undulations and depressions are accurately recorded, the underlying structure will be evident.

The difficulty is that such faithful rendering of every such detail in its proper relationship to other details and surfaces is very non-selective and pretty difficult too. How are you to decide which bump or depression is super-ficial and could in some instances be ignored, and which ones give evidence of the fundamental structure and are therefore probably more vital?

Some knowledge of human anatomy is therefore useful; enough at least to enable you to recognize those surface features which indicate the disposition of underlying structure.

To understand anatomy fully you should first begin with the bony skeleton, and the way it articulates, and then discover how cartilage, tendon and successive layers of muscle wrap the structure together, tension it and power the struts and levers to produce movement.

If your curiosity extends that far you will have to pursue it with the help of specialist anatomy books, several of which are listed in the bibliography, including the companion volume to this one.

Here and now I will try to simplify the whole thing by concentrating on identifying the major muscle groups and the tell-tale marks of the bony structure when it is very near the body surface. Recognition of these relatively few salient features will enable you to build a clear picture of the structure and dynamics of a pose.

In this section I have drawn (figs.1-5) schematic diagrams in which the basic struts, protective cages and boxes of the skeleton are sketched very lightly and the principle recognizable surface evidence of the skeleton is indicated by dark points and lines. We will call the latter the salient surface features.

From the back views the obvious primary clue to the posture of the figure is the long central depression which marks the spine, backbone or vertebral column. It is a depression and not a ridge because each side of it are muscular ropes which underly the surface muscles.

Near the surface and prominent in the upper back are the scapulae or shoulder blades. Although well covered by muscle layers, two features stand out and are useful in identifying shoulder movement. First are the scapula spines, raised ridges on the shoulder blades which angle to the outer upper corners to join via the shoulder girdles to the clavicles or collar bones in the front. These are seen at the surface as ridges or troughs depending on the individual's weight of surrounding musculature.

Secondly, the inner edges of the scapulae right down to their rather pointed lower angles, are normally easy to see. They are very useful pointers which are often misread, when as fig.3, the surrounding muscles are active and the edge becomes a groove.

Lower down the back the tilt of the hips or pelvis can be readily judged by reference to two points rather dauntingly named the posterior superior iliac crests/spines. They are often seen as prominent dimples in the female model, but may be slight protuberances in thin models of either sex. Together with the point at the base of the spine, they make a useful inverted triangle reference.

In the front of the torso the clavicles or collar bones, as already mentioned, are joined at their outer ends to a curved flat process (acromium) from the spine of the scapula to form the shoulder girdle.

Suspended from the backbone, the ribs

Fig.2

posterior iliac spines

Fig.3

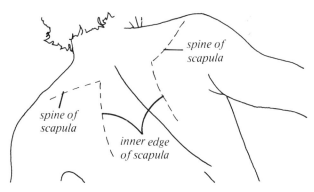

spine of scapula

spine of scapula

inner edge of scapula

61

Fig.4

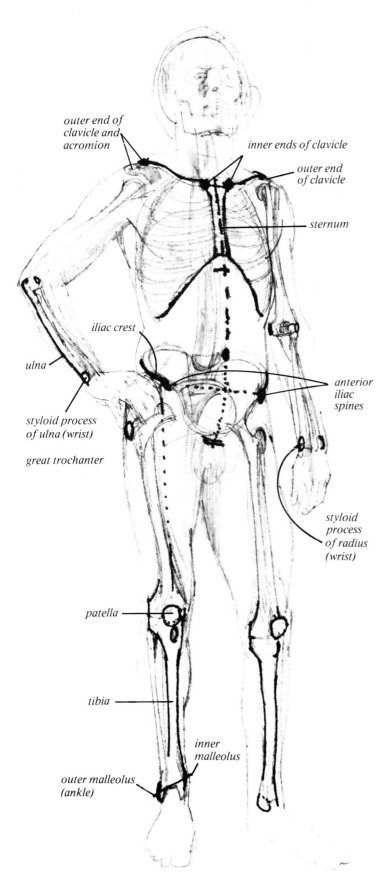

outer end of
clavicle and
acromion

inner ends of clavicle

outer end
of clavicle

sternum

iliac crest

ulna

styloid process
of ulna (wrist)

great trochanter

anterior
iliac
spines

styloid
process
of radius
(wrist)

patella

tibia

inner
malleolus

outer malleolus
(ankle)

curve around to the breast bone or sternum to form the thorax, a flexible cage, which by expansion and contraction activates the lungs and incidentally protects them and the heart and liver too.

The shape of the lower opening can usually be seen at the surface, especially the lower angles where the ribs change direction upwards to come together in an inverted 'V'.

Although the backbone is well hidden from the front, the centre line of the body can be traced by the line of the sternum continued down between the two vertical bands of muscles called the rectus abdominus to the pubis. The lower centre line is not always evident as the rectus abdominus plunges rather deeper there and fat tends to deposit there too.

The upper edges of the pelvis can usually be traced fairly clearly, and even more evident are the two angles of the pelvis called the 'iliac crests' or more properly the anterior superior iliac crests to differentiate them from the posterior superior iliac crests.

Visible from front, back and, with slightly

Fig.5

iliac crests

greater difficulty, from the side, are the great trochanters. In the female they are normally seen at the surface as bumps which mark the widest part of the hips. In males they are often hollows due to the bulk of muscle surrounding them and the different structure of the pelvis. The great trochanter is actually not a part of the pelvis at all, but a protuberance on the upper angles of the thigh bone or femur.

The remainder of the thigh bones run deep in the leg and only the lower end is seen at the surface where it swells out to meet and articulate with a similar shape at the top of the lower leg bone (tibia), so that together with the knee cap (patella), they form the rather angular shapes of the knee joint.

At the ankles the salient features are the inner and outer ankle bones (malleoli) which make characteristic downward sloping angles, the inner ankle higher than the outer.

Only at the elbow and wrist is there much evidence of the arm bones, although the major bone of the lower arm (ulna) is very near the surface for its whole length, and the upper

rounded end of the upper arm bone (humerous) does round out its muscle covering in a characteristic way.

The skull has been discussed already in the section Heads, Hands & Feet and the importance of its role in balance has been stressed. Its muscles are mainly comparatively small and used for pulling the surface tissues about to create expression, and do not greatly modify the overall form of the skull which remains the principal underlying structure to the face and head.

In the photographs on these pages I have indicated the main muscles or muscle groups on one side of the body by drawing them on the skin of the models.

If your model is amenable, I suggest you try to do the same, by reference to these photographs and the explanatory diagrams. Make-up pencils are ideal for this. The marks can be left there for the drawing session, a very interesting exercise, and they wash off fairly easily. A warning: some of the surface salient features are not as easily seen when you are

Fig.6

clavicles

sternum

iliac
crest

styloid
process
of ulna

Fig.7

patella

Fig.8

1 deltoid
2 serratus anterior
3 biceps (flexor group)
4 lower arm extensors
5 lower arm flexors
6 thigh extensors
7 lower leg extensors

8 iliac crest
9 patella
10 pectoral
11 thorax edge of lower
        opening
12 rectus abdominis

Fig.9

1 scapula spines
2 deltoid
3 infraspinatus
4 inner edge of scapula
5 trapezius

6 latissimus dorsi
7 iliac crest
8 posterior superior iliac
        crests

close to them, so in order to mark them it may
be necessary to feel for them, in some cases
delving quite hard to make certain of the
position of the bone. Make sure your model
understands this and doesn't mind.

A great advantage of drawing and photo-
graphing anatomy explanations on the skin of
the live model, is the infinity of views
available of the anatomization. The musculature
of the back is well known when viewed 'flat',
but it would be very difficult to predict the
foreshortened shapes seen from the views
represented by figs.8 and 9.

Although I have given the Latin names for
most of the important surface muscles of the
torso, I have named the muscles of the limbs

Fig.10

Fig.11

1 *scapula spine*	5 *inner edge of scapula*
2 *trapezius*	6 *scapula spine*
3 *posterior iliac spines*	7 *acromion*
4 *latissimus dorsi*	

1 *trapezius*	9 *calf flexors*
2 *deltoid*	10 *outer malleolus*
3 *triceps (extensors)*	11 *sterno mastoid*
4 *biceps (flexors)*	12 *clavicle*
5 *lower arm extensors*	13 *pectoral*
6 *ulna*	14 *rectus abdominis*
7 *iliotibial tract (flexors*	15 *iliac crest*
and extensors under)	16 *thigh extensors*
8 *thigh flexors*	17 *lower leg extensors*

as various groups of tensors or flexors.

Muscles in general terms act together in groups, either to bend the body or the limbs to which they are attached, in which case they are termed flexors, or to straighten or extend the same, when they are called extensors. It is convenient to name therefore the groups as 'arm extensors', 'thigh flexor group' etc., and it also helps you to know which muscles are likely to be tensed in any particular action. Tensor and flexor groups work together, the one giving way as the other contracts, so as to produce a controlled action, but the contracting group is always the more active and prominently enlarged.

65

Fig.1

Dynamics

Up to this point we have looked at the figure as a form with structure involving both hard and soft material, acted upon by the force of gravity. We have not yet considered the forces that are contained within the figure, which determine how the body resists or gives way to gravity. It may seem to be a matter of more interest to a physicist than an artist, but I hope to convince you that trying to discover what forms in the figure are doing, will add to your understanding of the way they *look*, and enable you to draw figures which, although not moving, are dynamic.

When I speak of a pose which is balanced but at rest, I mean one in which there is the minimum of muscular activity consistent with maintaining equilibrium, because of course, except in a completely relaxed lying position, some muscular power is always being applied.

In order for the figure to maintain equilibrium at rest, as we have seen, it has to arrange things so that the force of gravity on parts that could be pulled down to the ground, is absolutely equalized and balanced. It does this by delicately sensing a tendancy to be pulled one way, and immediately correcting the position by contracting one set of muscles, extending another set, until the balance is corrected, and then returning to rest.

The forms which are then in a sense stacked one above the other are each taking the weight of the forms above and transmitting the combined weight to those beneath and so on until ground contact is made. They are thus under compression.

A form which is suspended by a part or parts or itself will tend to be stretched, and it is therefore under tension.

It is a slightly misleading term in the context of figure drawing, as in a relaxed figure pose the forms which are subject to tension are being stretched, but only by their own weight, and consequently they appear slack and

Fig.2

comparatively soft, while those under compression will appear bunched and tense.

Consider the drawing (fig.2) on this page. Although the surface that is supporting the model is not drawn, it is clear from the pose that much of her weight is being supported by her elbows and most of the rest on the edge of the unseen surface.

Her upper arms are functioning as vertical props under compression, but relaxed, the pelvis similarly is firmly placed and pinned to the surface by its own weight. Her spine, compressed in a standing pose, is here suspended hammock-wise from a sling between the shoulder girdles, to the supporting plane at the pelvis. Her whole trunk is therefore at the same time stretched and sagging between the two supports, and her breasts rest on the suspended form, one softly spreading, the other just spilling over the edge.

Her legs are freely suspended from the supporting pelvis, supporting nothing but themselves. Her left leg, perhaps is not even doing this much; it seems to be held from the floor entirely by its stretched (under tension) connection to the hip.

It is some time since I made this drawing, and I can't remember what the model was supported on, or anything else about the circumstances, but looking at the drawing now, I know that what I liked about the pose and wanted to express were these dynamic tensions and compressions.

Dynamics

Project 1

For the first half of this session draw the model in clothes, in a standing pose with as much tilt and swing in it as can be managed. Exactly the same pose will be *unclothed* for the second half of the session.

A pose with the model's weight heavily on one leg with the opposite arm up and taking leaning weight, as here, is ideal for this exercise. Slightly loose garments, in a light-weight cloth in plain colours are best, so that they fall clearly into folds which reveal the directions of the body beneath. When drawing this figure pay particular attention to the pulls in the cloth, analysing where it is stretched i.e. under tension, and where and how it reacts to compression by folding on itself.

Human skin is much more elastic and flexible than clothing, and the pulls of tension and folds of extra material will not be as immediately obvious in the skin of the model when the same pose is adopted without clothes. Nevertheless something of the same thing *is* happening. Skin does fold when an area that it is covering is severely compressed, and it does have a stretched, taut look when the area is under tension.

You should try to find these areas which correspond to the tension and slackness in the clothing. Try to express the differences in tension by the way you draw; if a clue of thrust is sensed, draw it vigorously and assertively. Softer, slacker forms can be drawn more delicately with gently undulating lines or soft tones.

In fig.1 the main movement is shown by the way the cloth is pulled from the model's right elbow across and over the left hip. Note also the angle of the skirt hem line and bunched cloth above the left hand on hip.

Fig.3 clearly shows the straightness and strength of the left leg supporting the transferred weight of the figure via the bunched muscles of buttock and hip, the pelvis tilted leaving the right leg and buttock loose and relaxed (supported only by its own weight), and the resultant curve of the spine. Perhaps now return to the clothed pose and re-look. The line of the spine is no longer visible, the

Fig.1

pelvis tilt and the relative bunching and
relaxation of muscle groups cannot be seen
directly. Yet the pose is still immediately
readable because the looser envelope of the
clothing must react to the dynamics beneath.

It is essential to see and describe these
clothing folds in terms of what they are doing
and why, rather than solely copying their
shape. Work out which are the main directions
of stretch and try to figure out what underlying
form is responsible for it. Any linear medium
will do.

Fig.2

Fig.3

69

Fig.1

Dynamics

Project 2

For this project a chair with arms will be needed. The aim is to set up a really relaxed, almost reclining sitting pose, the model slumped deep into the chair, pelvis well forward, arms supported by arms of the chair.

In a sense the chair in this situation, takes over some of the function of the skeleton, functioning as a system of rigid supports for the flaccid forms of the figure.

Draw both chair and figure as one object in terms of rigidity and slackness.

This is a position frequently to be seen in gardens or on beaches in the summer, and I have included a drawing (fig.2) of my wife sunbathing in a beach chair in just the pose I have in mind. It was drawn some years ago, when we had time to take holidays!, and while I am not entirely happy with the drawing as a

Fig.2

whole, it does show fairly clearly, I think, the contrasting roles of rigid supports and relaxed suspensions. Even the beach chair itself is a model of the pose, being a system of struts and a slung canvas seat and back which falls to its limit under its own weight, and in this case, the weight of the figure too. Note how closely the curve of the spine, suspended between propped shoulder girdles and pelvis, follows the curve of the canvas, suspended between chair front rail and top rail. Of course they are to an extent forming each other, but given the same supports they would fall in a similar curve anyway.

Watch carefully for the way the shoulders are held up by the arm supports while the head and neck sinks with the slump of the body, and notice how the relaxed tissue is pulled downwards where it is unsupported by a surface e.g. the near thigh in fig.1 and the near upper arm.

Dynamics

Project 3

We return now to short poses. Positions which combine stretching, twisting, relaxation and tension are what is needed. Poses like this can only be held for short periods and it is essential to see the dynamics of the pose almost in one look. Try to see the *explanation* of the pose, the forces working within it, and see it *whole*. None of the drawings on this page took more than ten minutes, some only three or even just one minute.

This project and the one preceding, may seem to be repeating former projects. In some respects they are, and I make no apology for this. When drawing the dynamics of a figure, you will inevitably be involved in considering its weight and structure and balance too. It is just the emphasis that, for the purpose of each exercise, is expressly directed towards one aspect in particular.

There is always something new to discover about the human figure, and although there are only so many basic poses, there are infinite subtle variations.

You will find that in practice it is not always absolutely clear from the resulting drawing just what was the original motivation. But I think it is essential to have one, even if, as often happens, discoveries are made during the making of the drawing which lead to a shift

Fig.2

Fig.1

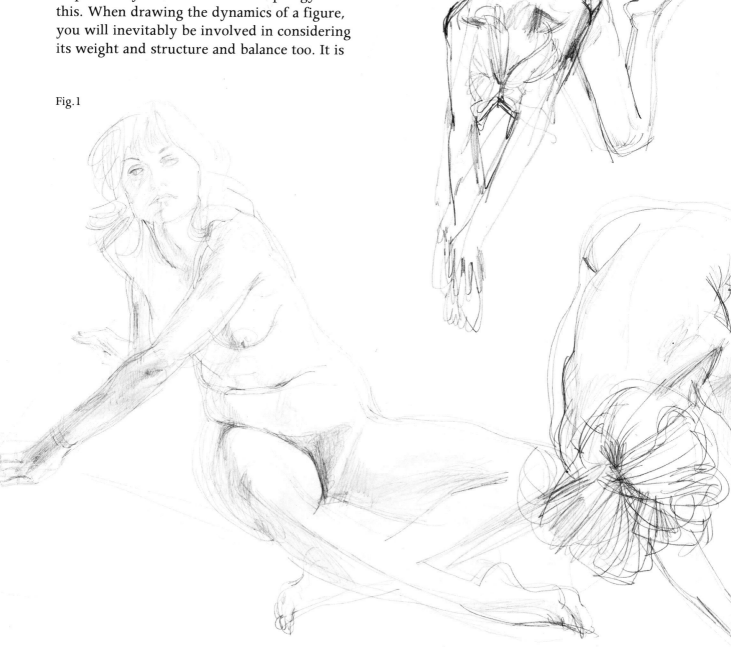

72

of emphasis. If you try to give too much information about too many aspects of the figure, you will say nothing clearly. This cannot be overstressed (however hard I try!).

By now you may feel confident to try making very quick drawings with pencil and pen as well as charcoal, and as long as you go for the essential action, there should be no need for erasure. Even when you have more time, you should not necessarily rub out construction lines or even gross errors.

You should not even think of errors at all in connection with drawing: every mark made is progress towards the final statement. If you make a mark, say a line denoting what seems to be the main direction of swing in one of those poses for example, and having decided that it is not quite right, rub it out, then you could quite easily put it back in the same place again. Better to leave it, and draw your later estimate alongside it. If that one seems right or nearer right as the drawing progresses, re-enforce it. The earlier lines will diminish by comparison, not affecting the final statement and yet by their presence showing how your thinking progressed.

Fig.3

Fig.5

Fig.4

73

Dynamics

Project 4

The most complete situation of tension in which a figure can be arranged, is that where the model is suspended by the hands, or of course the feet. Suspension from the feet has to be ruled out, and total suspension by the hands and arms cannot be maintained for longer than a very few minutes.

However, by providing the model with a secure high support that can be comfortably gripped by reaching up with the feet flat on the ground, a position of partial suspension can be held for periods of time long enough to make reasonable studies. About twenty minutes between rests is probably the most that should be expected.

When as in fig.1, both arms are used to suspend the figure, the whole of the torso is stretched and tensed. The weight of the body falling forward slightly has tensioned the arms so that they are stretched absolutely straight from the supporting bar. At the junction of the arm with the body, the muscles which surround and activate the shoulder joint are all stretched tightly too and this tension has to be expressed forcefully enough to match the strain of the

Fig.1

action. In this pose, and in nearly all partially suspended poses that can be held for long enough to draw, much of the body weight is being supported by one leg, only that weight which has been allowed to pivot onto the relaxed other side being in reality held by the arms.

The pelvic tilt will therefore be obvious, as it was in the standing pose showing weight shift, but with the vital difference that equilibrium is not maintained by counterswing, but by suspension. Note how far the head is offset from a position vertically above the weight-taking heel.

Single-handed suspension of course puts the suspended side of the torso into tension, allowing the other side to relax, the main body weight being transferred via the pelvis to the leg away from the suspending arm. The other leg is relaxed to allow the tilted weight to hang from the straight arm.

The top of a door, or a robust easel will do for the one-handed pose. The other one will require a firmly fixed bar or crosspiece, perhaps bridging between two ladders.

Fig.2

Dynamics

Project 5

For this project, explore less strained ways of posing the model, in which stretched and compacted, propped and suspended forms can perhaps be more subtly analysed.

Stretching without undue strain can be achieved by reclining poses on undulating or stepped surfaces. The model in fig.2 for example is lying with her legs and pelvis on the raised, mattress-covered surface of the model's throne, and her 'upper' body has been allowed to fall to the floor level. If the levels are carefully adjusted, the pose can be reasonably comfortable, and yet as you can see the downward stretching of the abdomen leaves a tense hollow between the jutting hipbones and pubis, which contrasts with the relaxed upper body forms which have come to rest at the bottom of the slope.

Fig.2, shows a variation on the slumped seating poses of project 2 in this section but here the arms are supporting more weight and pushing the shoulders up to their limit. This extreme 'shrug' position only occurs if the model relaxes; it is quite easy for the shoulder and chest muscles to pull the body up on the propped shoulders so that the head and neck are raised, but this is then a position of strain, the muscles soon tire and the 'shrug' position is resumed.

Another pose which is interesting in this context is that shown in fig.1 in which the lower body is curled into a compacted shape supported over a wide area, while the upper body is suspended between pelvis and cradled arms. There are many variations of this pose, and as with all the suggestions you must find the position which suits the model and the circumstances and best expresses the movement that you want. A variation which comes to mind, but is not illustrated, would need the model to be kneeling up more so that the spine and all the soft torso hanging from it, was suspended more completely as a bridge.

Fig.1

Fig.2

Fig.3

77

Light and shade

There are occasions when the most interesting and visually arresting fact of a figure in situation is not its solidity, its structure, its dynamics, all of which are seen by virtue of the light which falls on it, but the pattern of the light itself.

Up to this point, we have used tone, if at all, as a means of creating the illusion of solidity. Mostly it has corresponded with shadow areas observed on the figure. But not all the shadow areas have necessarily been recorded. Only tone which is necessary to explain form needs to be used, and the depth of that tone need not always match that of the observed shadow area. Moreover, if the areas of shadow or tones of light are judged not sufficient to clarify form or movement, tones can be invented to do the job.

As I have said, linear outlines are inventions; no such line can be seen in reality, it is just a useful and well understood part of the complete visual language.

Now we will look specifically at the figure in terms of light and shade only. Lines

Fig.1

78

representing the edges of objects need not be used. Edges, which after all, only represent the disappearance from view of the outside planes of an object, can just as well be represented by a change of tone as by a line. If there *is* no discernable tonal change, as is sometimes the case, the edge can be *inferred* from adjacent edges that *can* be seen tonally.

In fact one of the excitements of light and shade is ambiguity of outline, now you see it, now you don't, and the artist can use this to advantage. Attention can be directed to selected areas of the drawing by, almost literally, spotlighting it, and whole areas can be lost in shadow to reinforce the emphasis.

So there is still a place for selectivity and exaggeration in drawing light and shade – we are using our eyes to see what the camera records, but we can choose what we use.

Fig.2

Fig.3

Some line may be used initially to define outer edges, but increasingly you should look instead for the edges of tonal areas, defining these and treating the edges of the figure as of secondary importance unless they are represented by strong contrasts of tone.

It follows of course, that using tonal changes to define outer edges, implies judging and representing the background all round the figure, and this will lead into compositions which place the figure in an environment.

Also completely tonal drawing, where no line is used, only areas of light and shade, comes close to being painting. In fact it is difficult to decide at just what point one becomes the other. Painting has often been described as 'drawing with paint', so perhaps there is no really intrinsic difference.

In the Composition section there will be more on the subject of the figure and background, and 'drawing with paint'.

Light and shade

Project 1

Arrange the model in any convenient pose lit by a single light source so as to produce strong definition between light and shade.

It is not the easiest situation to organize, as it is necessary not only to light the model in the right way but also to ensure adequate light to draw by.

If the light in your studio is natural sunlight it is probably best to place the model near to the window so that maximum contrast in lighting can be achieved, and then choose your position rather further from the light source so that plenty of shadow area can be seen in the figure. There will probably be sufficient reflected light from a wall to illuminate your drawing surfaces.

In artificial light, it is a little trickier. A photographic flood lamp or even a spot is ideal, but failing that a reflector lamp in an anglepoise or similar movable light would do. Failing *that*, placing the model near to a low and directional overhead light will have to do.

Depending on how many people are drawing, more directional light will have to be procured to light the drawing surfaces without spilling light onto the model and spoiling the strongly defined light and shade areas.

When all is arranged, look at the model, maybe half close your eyes to merge detail and minor light changes, and try to see, not form, not weight, not dynamics, not structure, but light and shade.

Assess the relative depth of shadow areas one to another, and decide which of the basically light areas is really the very lightest.

For the moment line can be used to help find the outline, but start thinking about a light edge where it gives way to a dark

Fig.1

80

background as just that – a change of tone, and draw it so.

Treat this project as an 'easing in' to the idea of light and shade.

It may not be so very different from drawings you have made previously; it depends on how much tone you habitually use.

The vital difference is that, while previously you should have been using tone only where necessary to clarify what you were searching for, now it is the tone itself that should concern you, its area, its depth, the pattern made by it and the light areas.

Fig.3

Fig.2

Light and shade

Project 2

More dramatic lighting than last time is needed for this project. If the model is posed standing or sitting directly under a bright light source, the tops of forms will be strongly lit and will cast dark shadows on lower forms. Minor adjustments of position under the light will produce big changes in the lighting situation, so a pose should be chosen which can be maintained without swaying or gradual sagging.

Fig.1

In this lighting situation, every form is thrown into sharp relief, and the head and neck, being closest to the light source tend to be particularly dramatically transformed.

Even in the most dramatic light however, the dark areas of shade receive some degree of reflected light, the darkest parts often being nearest to where the shadow gives way to light.

This apparent darkening of shadow areas where they meet the bright light areas, is an interesting phenomenon and vital to appreciate.

As I have said, it is partly, perhaps mainly, a result of the tone furthest from the light on a rounded form, being in the best position to catch light from the main source reflected back into it from nearby lit forms.

In addition however, the eye adds to the effect by seeing adjacent contrasting tones, as more contrasting than they objectively are.

This can be verified by reference to fig.2. Here the areas of contrasting tone are themselves absolutely flat and even, but your eye will tell you that they are not. Each tone seems to graduate to give maximum contrast at the junctions. Isolation of any one tone by masking with paper will show that the tones really are flat.

In practice this accenting of the line of change from light to dark is very helpful. If this 'edge' is searched out and put down accurately, the rest of the shadow tone can to a certain extent look after itself. The solidity of the form in light and the feeling of strong light is more dependent on the place *where* light changes to shade than by how *much* it changes. So, search out the shapes of the areas of light and shade; they should in the main be sharply defined.

Fig.2

Fig. 3

Light and shade

Project 3

Light illuminating the figure from below always creates an unexpected, unfamiliar appearance.

I am referring of course, to lighting which is from a low level relative to the upright figure; the same effect can be achieved by lighting the prone figure from the feet end. The model's torso in fig.2 is almost upside down so that the same lighting is produced by nearly overhead lighting, the unusual appearance being heightened by the effect of gravity pulling the forms the 'wrong' way.

You should by now, be beginning to make judgements about *all* the tones, not just those on the figure itself. This means much greater areas of paper to be covered and thought should be given to the choice of media.

Given sufficient time, tone can be created with great subtlety by the use of pen line or dot, but in the time normally available with a live model it is not very practical.

Pastel, chalk, crayon and the ubiquitous charcoal are quicker and more malleable.

Ideally you need, not only to work from light to dark, but also to be able to add to and change light areas, even if it is achieved by erasing or moving tonal areas. Charcoal and

Fig.1

Fig.2

Fig.3

putty rubber (or bread which works well) is
ideal for the latter method, but in order actually
to apply light areas you will have to use white
chalk or coloured pastels.

Elevating the model on a table or similar
raised surface as in fig.3, facilitates lighting the
standing figure from a low level and allows
more background possibilities. In this case the
head and parts of the shoulders are virtually
the same tone as the background. In such
instances, when figure and background merge
tonally, let them do so; such uncertainties add
to the excitement of tonal studies, as do
counterchanges where a tone is at one point a
light against dark, and elsewhere, although
tonally unchanged becomes suddenly, by
virtue of a background variation, a dark
against light.

Look for pattern as ever, organize the shapes
by reference to your mind's eye vertical/
horizontal grid and try to keep the drawing
mobile to the end.

85

Fig. 2

Light and shade

Project 4

In this session I suggest that you take one step further towards a purely tonal representation of the figure in a situation. Pose the model in a shadowy corner, and shed just enough light to catch some of the major forms.

The actual position adopted is not important, but sitting or reclined poses usually give more interesting patterns of light and shade than standing ones.

If the lighting is selective and dim enough, the figure will emerge from the surrounding gloom by virtue of a relatively few well lit forms, much of the edges of the figure being lost or hard to define. If these light areas on the figure and those on surrounding surfaces, are well judged in their positions, shape and relative brightness, a great deal of the rest of the figure which is lost in shadow, will be easily inferred by the viewer.

Fig. 1

Fig.3

Try to rid yourself therefore of the need to represent outer edges by line at all; let the tones speak for themselves. This applies to edges of limbs within the external outline of the figure. There is an example of what I mean in the drawing fig.3 where the model's right calf rest over her left knee. The adjacent forms are both lit quite well, so they have been allowed to merge with just a small change of tone between them. Their sharing of the sparse amount of available light is more important than the fact that in different circumstances they will become quite separate forms.

Colour too, and pattern need to be considered in tonal drawings. When drawing form and structure, the local colour of tissue, colour of hair and surrounding surfaces and forms, is of no importance and can deflect your attention from the point of the drawing. Drawing light and shade purely means that you have to give a tonal value to *all* the surface, so that colours which although receiving light are themselves tonally dark, must be represented so.

Fully tonal drawings are rather rare in the history of art, perhaps because of the afore-mentioned proximity to painting, but I recommend you to look at the Seurat on page 144, to see how light and shade can be handled completely without line and yet remain unarguably a drawing.

Clothing

It may sometimes be wondered at that so much figure drawing is done from the nude model, when in real life most people are almost always to be seen more or less clothed.

The main reason, I believe, is that the nude human figure is the supreme test of draughtsmanship. Not that it is necessarily *the* most difficult subject that exists, but it is the subject that most ruthlessly exposes dishonesty, laziness or plain ineptitude. There are just too many people who will know immediately if a drawing of the nude is basically right or wrong for you to be able to get away with slack drawing.

A tree can be drawn grossly inaccurately and few people will know; only experts know if machines, plants, animals are really well drawn and even they tend to check details rather than subtle proportion and form, but we have a very critical eye for our own kind.

Not many people can use their subliminal sense of the 'rightness' of a figure to draw well themselves; that, as we have seen, needs a new objective vision, and few can always pinpoint exactly what failure of objective vision has made a drawing look wrong. Some flashy techniques may confuse criticism for a while, but not for long. Honesty shines through good figure drawing for all to see, dishonesty cannot be concealed.

As a result it is generally agreed that drawing the nude figure embodies *all* the disciplines and problems as well as the challenge and excitement of drawing anything.

Having said all this, I feel there is another reason.

Even if all you ever wanted to draw were people in clothes it would still be better to explore and understand the figure *beneath* the clothes first.

Clothes are made to fit the human body; they are not always a close fit, but always they are supported and activated by the structure, form and dynamics of the body they cover. They can be thought of as extra, looser skins, and they have to react and accommodate themselves to the movement of the figure in a similar way. It follows that to understand the stresses involved in the human skin covering will help your understanding of the way clothing behaves.

It is also true that analysis of what would be called the dynamics of clothing, where lack of the elasticity of skin renders the tensions and slackness grosser and easier to read, can help you to sort out the dynamics of the underlying figure.

The following projects in this section therefore, will suggest ways of exploring and clarifying the relationship between the nude figure and clothing, and understanding the dynamics of clothing itself.

Fig.1

Fig.2

Fig.3

89

Fig.1

Clothing

Project 1

For this exercise you will require a bed sheet or similar size piece of plain fabric. Sitting or reclining poses wrapped in this fabric can then be arranged so that there is a good variety of folded and stressed fabric. The situation to be aimed for is a combination of falling folds, crumpled fabric and tightly stressed forms.

The primary objective now is to make studies of the fabric, trying to discover its form, but with especial attention paid to the type of forms which result from the various combinations of gravity and support.

For example, in fig.1, fabric supported by the model's knee is first stretched tight and smooth over the upper surface of the knee, then at the edges of the supporting form the fabric falls into nearly straight-downwards folds until it meets the top of a foot or the floor, when if there is sufficient length it folds upon itself in a variety of nearly random shapes. I say nearly random, because although at first sight fabric seems to fall into an infinity of different unconnected shapes, in fact given similar conditions of stress and support from

Fig.2

90

Fig.3

underlying forms, fabrics of similar weight, texture etc., tend to react in a predictable way.

Details of folds may differ each time the cloth in a given situation is picked up and dropped again, but the *type* of folding especially over the stress points will increasingly be recognized as typical.

You may notice in this drawing that the nearest forms are drawn darker and with greater stress than the forms farther back, which achieves a feeling of recession. This is not an entirely conscious device. Indeed, such things never work if they are premeditated. During a drawing all effort is concentrated on discovering the uniqueness of the object, and using whatever marks that may seem necessary at the time.

Once the marks describe your discovery accurately and clearly, no addition or embellishment is necessary. If they do not describe accurately or are ambiguous they should be changed, and changed until it all works as well as one's capability permits. This is the natural process of drawing. The areas which are giving the most trouble or which seem to be most vital, are changed and returned to again and again, and acquire a more worked on look.

This is how you get the areas of greater stress – they reflect the draughtsman's dwelling of attention; the progress of the search can be traced.

There are occasions in the best-organized life drawing group when for one reason or another you may find yourself without a model for a session. This particular project is a useful one in these circumstances, as a couple of chairs with the fabric draped and wrapped over them will do almost as well as the model as a basis for your studies.

Clothing

Project 2

Have the model wear a loose fitting garment
such as a dressing gown. The fabric should be
plain, preferably fairly light coloured and of a
thin, clinging consistency which makes good
folds but hugs forms quite closely too. The
objective of this exercise is to discover the
figure underneath the cloth through the
stresses visible in the garment.

    In fig.1 the pose is intentionally simple and
undramatic and the garment is fairly loose and
shapeless. Because the model's knees and lower
legs are uncovered and the contact points of
the chair legs and her feet are clearly visible,
the basis of the structure can be established
without reference to the clothing. Thereafter
clues to the underlying form must be sought
in the folds and stress lines of the garment.

Fig.1

Fig.2

Because it is a garment, not just a fabric wrapping as in project 1, the clues are somewhat different, but there are plenty of them. Note the way that the direction of pulls from the lowest front fastening of the gown describes the flat plane across her lap and turns to join other curved folds following the rounded form of her thigh. The pockets are bulged out by her hands, the weight of hand and arm pulling folds from the shoulders and helping to define the front plane of her chest. Smooth areas above the breast, undulating, slightly crumpled forms beneath tell of the fullness of breasts and slimmer but quite round middle. Sleeves fall from shoulders and are then forced to fold deeply in the bend of the arms – all the main directions of the body can be deduced.

In fig.2 the form of the garment has been searched out with greater concentration on the appearance and quality of the folding of the fabric, but still plenty of information about the pose comes through. The long waist tie, not only defines the waist, but by trailing down the abdomen and then over the near thigh delineates these forms too.

Such garment details as collars, arm seams, back and side seams can often be used to help to define forms in a similar way, as we will see in the next project.

Clothing

Project 3

We come now to garments which are designed to fit the figure more closely, which may be multi-layered but which must allow the figure normal freedom of movement. As you would expect, there are many more seams and much less fabric free-falling into long sweeping folds.

Ask the model to wear normal underclothes, a jacket and skirt or trousers, shoes and socks etc., preferably plain, not too dark coloured materials again, so that the dynamics of folding can be clearly seen. Choose fairly normal sitting poses as here, remembering that if a pose is difficult to hold requiring very frequent rests, the folding of the material will be different after every rest. As I said in the introduction to this section, this does not mean that the *type* of folding will be intrinsically changed each time the pose is resumed, one can learn to draw a sort of stress pattern which represents the function of a set of folds rather than their precise shapes, but it's nice to get a few typical fold forms into your visual memory from explicit observation first.

For the purpose of this exercise, which is to discover more about the stress patterns of clothing that reveal its structure and that of the body beneath, I think that you should not pay too much attention to garment detailing for its own sake.

The number of teeth in a zip fastener for instance is not important, but the direction it takes is. A line of stitching that by its direction defines a form or reveals tension is important, but purely decorative stitching is not. Do not misunderstand me; in another context, decorative stitching, pattern and colour could quite legitimately be your primary interests.

Note that in fig.2 the pocket seams on her jacket have helped to establish the side plane. The seam of the arm hole explains the discontinuity of the jacket fold resulting from the forward thrust of the arms, and those over the upper arm and shoulder. Also the side seam of her jeans tells of how the tube of cloth has had to fold on itself in the inside of the bent knees, while in fig.3, the side seam's discontinuity shows how much the loose cloth of his trouser leg is displaced.

Fig.1

Use tone where necessary to explain form and function but not to denote colour. That's a waste of time in this context. Shoes are only a problem if you let your preconceptions of what shoes are like, based usually on the profile view, get in the way of your objective vision of the often encountered foreshortened views.

Fig.2

Clothing

Project 4

This project explores further what was begun in Dynamics project 1, that is, the analysis of a standing pose by reference to clothing.

Basically loose clothing which is close fitting at the waist, such as the long skirt in fig.4, most dramatically reveals the nature and degree of weight shift in a standing pose, by so accurately conforming where it can free-fall, to the pull of gravity.

It makes visible the invisible canopy of forces I have asked you to imagine.

I suggest that you extend this exercise over more than one session in order to make a series of drawings of standing poses variously clothed.

Minimal clothing, amounting to little more than a framing shape, as in fig.5, can add interest to a heavily asymmetrically weighted pose by providing a vertical reference to measure the movement against.

The backward swing of the jacket in fig.1 helps to dramatize the balance of the pose.

I have also included two drawings from life of a fashion model (figs.2 and 3). Fashion

Fig.1　　　　　Fig.2　　　　　Fig.3

drawings represent a very specialized area of clothed figure drawing, in that it is the garments which are of first importance and the figure is expected to conform to the designer's idea of the shape of his clothes rather than the other way round.

Consequently the distortions of the figure vary in a degree and kind dependent on the currently preferred outline and how far the fashion illustrator is expected to go in fantasising on the theme.

The most constant adjustment generally considered to make clothes look good, is an elongation of the figure so that the head length which is normally about one sixth to one seventh of the total height, goes instead into the body ten, twelve or many more times.

My two drawings, while not being finished fashion illustrations, but just the preliminary drawings from life, have nevertheless been consciously elongated in this way.

There is much more to fashion figure drawing of course than this brief exposition has told, but it *is* very specialized and rather subjective, and therefore strictly outside the declared limits of this book.

Fig.4

Fig.5

Character

In order to define what I mean by character in this context, I think it easiest to recall first what we have been looking for in the previous projects.

I have suggested that you consider shape, weight, balance, structure, anatomy, dynamics, light and shade, clothing – all abstract concepts Even in the section on head, hands and feet I have concentrated on objective, abstract elements. Nowhere have I encouraged you to think of your model as a person. I believe that it has been a necessary constriction. Cezanne's famous advice that a head should be painted as though it was an apple, is an example of the same thinking. To be able to 'see' objectively requires an initial denial of the mass of visual half-truths that we have acquired through social contact and interaction, and its replacement by concentrated objective observation of each form as though it had never been seen before. The point has been made often enough I hope, and I will not labour it further.

A point will eventually be reached however, when the habit of direct analytical observation will have become, if not entirely second nature, at least fairly natural to slip into when settling down to draw. I suggest that now is the time to allow yourself to re-admit some of the originally denied emotional reactions to the model as a person. All the other objective realities have still to be dealt with, but you should in addition, try to discover what makes the human figure that you are drawing specially different from any other.

The face of course is where we normally expect to find the identity of a particular individual, and it is true that we gain a lot of information about current mood and personality traits from looking at the face. But we *recognize* people from distances and angles where the facial expression and details are not discernable. The essential recognizable character of an individual is there in the whole body.

It is this that I suggest you now try to search out. I would not expect the drawings

necessarily to look vastly different – particular 'likeness' still resides in shape and proportion – but the emphasis should be different.

Searching out small asymmetries, where symmetry is to be expected, noting the imperfections or unusual colourations of hair or skin, or any other features which are distinctive and special to the person who is your subject. Be prepared to exaggerate these features a little or a lot, and to subjugate or ignore some of the objective features of form, structure and so on.

It is not easy. It is especially difficult to combine this 'humanity' with still, strong objective drawing, but it is very satisfying when it works.

Character

Project 1

Ask your model to adopt a pose which both looks to you and feels to the model, to be natural and comfortable.

It may be that during a rest period in a drawing session, you will catch the model off guard, relaxing unselfconsciously into an attitude which is more natural and typical than the poses which have been formally arranged.

On the other hand, if the model has been a regular sitter for you or your group, there may be poses which you particularly liked in earlier sessions which you feel could be drawn again with a different emphasis.

To catch the essential character it is generally helpful to have a view of the face, the strongest connection being made between viewer and model when there is direct eye to eye contact. This is the situation when the eyes in portraits are said to 'follow you round the room', and you do receive an enhanced sense of there being a real person there, when the eyes are looking straight at you.

However, it is not essential and not possible for everyone if you are drawing in a group. In any case you should not limit your search for character to the face of the sitter alone;

shoulders and upper body or the whole figure should contribute to the complete impression.

Some consideration of the immediate surroundings of the sitter establishes the figure in a real place, rather than the limbo of a figure study on a white page, and helps to create the feeling of there being a real person inside. If the model holds a book or a cup, or is knitting, it can help to reinforce the naturalness of a pose too.

When drawing, look for proportion and form as before but with an especial eye to discovering what makes this particular person different from others.

I repeat that it is only a slight change in emphasis. It means that when you draw, for example, a hand and arm, it is not enough that it should be a well drawn arm, with solidity, weight and good tension or slackness; it should also look like this *particular* hand and arm. If by delving too deeply into its structure, you have destroyed its delicacy, then in this context, you have failed. On the other hand, if the character of the same hand and arm is there but the form or solidity are a little lacking it may be all right. The essential thing is to make sure the whole drawing hangs together – some inaccuracies and exaggerations are permissible as long as the figure is all of a piece and says something about the uniqueness of the person you are drawing.

Fig.1

Fig.3

Fig.2

Fig.1

Character

Project 2

This project is another one that can be kept in reserve against the possibility of being without a model for a session. There are three possibilities, assuming that you are drawing as a group.

First each member of the group can take a turn at posing for the others. Each pose should be short enough to allow everyone to do their share of posing within the session. As this means you probably won't have very much time to make each drawing, economy of means is essential. If all your sketches are on one pose, you will be able to see whether you have been able to capture the variety of character and expression rather than drawing a succession of stereotyped heads.

Another way is to all draw each other simultaneously. This is not as complex as it sounds. If you all sit, or stand, in a widely spaced group, each person can choose to draw any other, and may themselves be drawn by the same person or any other. Of course all the drawings will be of people drawing and so there will be a certain amount of movement involved. The shifts in position tend to be minor, however, chiefly confined to looking up at the model and down at drawing alternately, and occasional easing of a position

Fig.2

Fig.3

for a slight rest. If you choose to draw the
position which is most frequently adhered to
and ignore the occasional lapses, there should
be no problem. At least your subject will know
that he is being drawn and will try to keep
movement to the minimum. If you draw people
that you see about you in everyday life, as I
think you should, there is no guarantee that
any position will be maintained for more than
a few minutes or even seconds, so it is essential
to develop the ability to see a face or figure in
one look and to put down the essentials in a
very few strokes.

The third alternative for this project is to
draw a self portrait. For this of course you
must have a mirror, large enough if possible
to be able to see the whole of your figure in
one view. Your most available model is after
all yourself and although the necessity to be
in a position to draw and yet be able to see
yourself in a mirror is a trifle limiting, you will
find that with some ingenuity a large number of
poses *are* possible. Two large mirrors can be
placed so that even back views can be seen and
drawn. A great deal can be learned from self-
portraiture; for many artists it has been a
constantly recurring theme, sometimes
combining the self portrait with other figures
seen in the mirror.

You may find it interesting to draw yourself
from the mirror with one or more other figures,
or dressed in a variety of costumes.

Fig.5

Fig.6

Fig.4

Character

Project 3

I have throughout the preceding sections made
no mention of the possibilities of drawing
from more than one model at a time.

Perhaps I have been remiss by the omission,
but I have been conscious of the difficulty
and the cost of arranging sessions with two or
more models. If you have pursued the course
so far though, you may have acquired a number
of model contacts and have enough enthusiastic
members of your drawing group to be able to
consider hiring or persuading two people to
pose together.

The interest and possibilities are heightened
enormously, whatever the area of interest, by
the juxtaposition of two figures. The composite
shapes and volumes which are made by the two
figures in contact or even entwined as one,
seem almost limitless. There is the added

Fig.1

Fig.2

bonus that the 'two headed monster' is an unfamiliar shape and therefore more likely to be drawn without preconception.

Placing the figures physically apart but connected by line of sight, or by compositional tensions (more of this in the section on Composition) opens up further possibilities, and it hardly needs to be said that the introduction of more figures, singly or in groups, expands the permutations to infinity.

For the purposes of this particular exercise you should choose as models, two people of dissimilar type and/or age. The greater the contrast between them the easier will be the task of stressing the differences, but you may enjoy the challenge of discovering the more subtle disparities between similar types.

My two models in the drawings here, while contrasting strongly in terms of bulk and age, seem to be rather similar facially, almost as mother and daughter although they are in fact unrelated.

The drawing of the model with a plaster cast of the Venus de Milo records non-intentional juxtaposition which occurred in the liferoom of an art school, at the time when it was standard practice to surround students with many such greco-roman casts. Most of the great draughtsmen have spent some time drawing from the 'antique'. Unfortunately during the Victorian period in England, the practice of drawing from these plaster casts became so laboriously pursued with such painstaking attention to detailed and highly photographic, rather sterile, rendering that the practice fell into disrepute. As a result very few of these lovely plaster casts are to be found outside the museums nowadays. If there are any accessible to you I suggest that it would be rewarding to go and make some drawings of them, if only to underline the differences between the classical view of the figure and

Fig.3

your own observation of real life. I found the extreme contrast of the sharp forms of the ex-stripper model and the rounded idealism of the Venus, not to mention the enormous size differential, to be rather amusing.

105

Character

Project 4

Elderly people are always interesting to draw, and are obviously particularly suitable when exploring character.

Habitual expressions gradually become etched on faces as the skin grows less elastic, producing the tracery of lines associated with old age. Revealing though these patterns are of character, if you can persuade an elderly person to pose for you, you will discover that there is more to ageing than superficial creasing.

Allow your elderly model to adopt a pose which is comfortable and natural. Try to establish a relaxed atmosphere, converse with your model, watch carefully and only begin to draw when you are sure that the model is not consciously posing and is truly relaxed.

Fig.1

Fig.2

You will find that there will be something about the whole attitude that expresses the age and character of your sitter. Try to analyse this and either establish it first or have it in your mind as you start with the head.

When analysing the face, look for the bony structure of the skull which is often much more prominent in an elderly person, due to slacker tissue and musculature. In many cases atrophy of the lower jaw, especially where most or all of the natural teeth have been lost, contributes to further looseness of tissue around the jaw and neck.

Observe the way the head is held – it may be excessively upright or bowed, but nearly always different from the posture of a young person. Hands and arms too are revealing. Joints in elderly people are often arthritic and enlarged, and seem more so because the musculature has atrophied.

Watch how the clothes hang and what they tell you of the forms beneath. Shoulders, elbows, knees, may be sharper, the chest hollower, abdomen rounder.

On the other hand none of this may apply – I seem to be creating a preconception of total decrepitude – your model may present a picture of blooming health and robustness.

The essential thing is to be looking beyond and beneath the wrinkles to search out more fundamental character features.

Fig.3

107

Movement

Mobility in the human figure has always posed special problems for the artist.

Before the discovery of photography the only way to draw a figure in the course of violent action was to remember a fleeting momentary glimpse, relate it to the positions at the beginning and the end of the action, and hope that it was somewhere near right. Poses in mid-action could be simulated of course, and held long enough for studies to be made, but such simulations always lack conviction.

The problem is that locomotion on two legs at the most gentle rate is only possible by successively losing balance and regaining it.

This can readily be appreciated by considering what happens when running or walking if the leg which is *not* taking the weight of the body at any given moment, is prevented from moving forward to take *its* turn at supporting – the body crashes to the ground. Running is falling forwards, being caught and pushed forwards onto another potential fall and caught again by the other leg and so on, until the decision is made to stop, when the forward fall is arrested and equilibrium resumed.

It follows that any attempt to hold a pose representing any frozen moment of the action is impossible because it must be a position of total imbalance. Various supports can be devised to enable a basically unbalanced position to be maintained, but this can never be entirely satisfactory, as the dynamics of the body adjust to the newly introduced props, achieving static balance again which is just what running is not.

Slower action *can* be analysed by eye as I will explain in the first project, but really fast ones can only be guessed at or suggested by

Fig.1

drawing the static beginning or end of the movement.

When the figure leaves the ground altogether, as in jumping, there is just no possibility of making any thorough analysis of the action by eye. Again guesses can be made and universally accepted conventions established for representing certain actions. Horses depicted with the front legs stretched forwards together and the back legs backward, were accepted for centuries as galloping, until high speed photography revealed how the legs really moved in the gallop.

It has to be admitted that artists of the past have made better guesses about the movement of the human figure than they did about the horse, movable models helping in this respect no doubt. Such models range from very simplified to beautifully shaped and articulated versions of the human figure. Usually made of wood and supported somewhere around their centre of gravity, they can be easily manipulated into a great variety of active poses, some possible in reality, some impossible. By experimenting a little it is possible to come up with some convincing looking simulations of actions. However they lack dynamics and I am

not sure whether the sense of conviction engendered is not due to the memory of a photographic version of the action – i.e. *before* photography there would have been no correct visual idea to match with the lay figure. The models were probably not developed for the purpose of simulating action anyway. Their primary use was as life size substitutes for the live subjects of portraiture. Clothed in the appropriate garments they would be left in the chosen position indefinitely while the robes and regalia were painted, the important sitter only requiring to be present when the painting of head, hands etc. was undertaken.

So, it seems, if we are to draw movement in these days when the frozen photographic instant is commonplace, we really have no alternative, at least for the speedier actions, but to turn to photographs for information.

The succeeding projects suggest how you can make best use of them.

Fig.2

Movement

Project 1

Even an action as seemingly simple as walking was not fully understood until sequence photography made it possible to analyse every stage of the movement. Curiously enough the same kind of analysis *is* possible without the use of the camera.

First ask your model to walk across the studio slowly, turn and walk back again and repeat this sequence continuously. Take any moment in this continuous action and try to freeze some small feature of it in your memory. Draw that feature, wait for the exact moment of the movement to be repeated and note

Fig.2

Fig.1

A Muybridge sequence of photographs.

Nude descending a staircase, No. 2. 1912, by Marcel Duchamp. This representation of movement was specifically inspired by Muybridge's photographs. Philadelphia Museum of Art, Pennsylvania. The Louise and Walter Arensberg Collection.

another feature. The sort of things to look for are pelvis swing, head carriage, shoulder tilt, weight distribution and balance shift indicated by position of head over weight-taking foot.

A picture of one instant of the action can be built up in this way.

Next a succeeding moment in the action can be observed and recorded in the same way, and then another, as long as you and your model's stamina lasts.

If you have analysed accurately and in sequence it will be obvious that walking is a succession of changes of balance and imbalance, a sort of falling forward over each succeeding supporting leg. In the first drawing of my sequence (fig.1), the weight is just shifting to the right leg, and at this moment the right shoulder is dropped to achieve balance as the left leg is swung forward. The head is well forward of the weight-taking foot, so we know that the figure is about to fall forward. As it does so the left leg has finished its forward swing and taken up the duty of main support as in stages 2 and 3, the left shoulder dropping to allow the right leg in turn to swing forward. Since it is a slow walk the arms are fairly static, but in faster action they swing forward with alternate legs.

Subsequently two lines have traced the movement of the functionally vital points of shoulder and hip, and show how they rise and fall alternately in a fluid motion.

It won't be possible for you to make very finished or detailed drawings this way; it does require quite intense observation just to produce little sketches like these, but the exercise helps real understanding of the action and speeds up your reactions.

You should find it interesting to compare your results with the Muybridge photographic series. If you didn't manage to make an on-the-move analysis, try analysing the movement by copying the photo sequence. The Marcel Duchamp painting, reproduced on this page, was an attempt to reproduce movement that was specifically inspired by Muybridge photographs.

Fig.3

Movement

Project 2

For this project and the next one a live posed model will not be needed. Instead, collect mid-action photographs of running and jumping athletes from magazines or newspapers or any other available source.

Having found a sharp photograph of an instant of an action, you could of course just look at it and draw from it, tone for tone, until you have produced a facsimile, but this would be a pointless exercise. There must be some selection of the information and some statement made about the action. To do this, you need to be able to understand the complete action of which you are to draw a small part.

In order to understand the action of running, you will need a number of photographs so that all stages of the action, and several views and types of individual, are depicted.

Sort your collection into groups of similar views and try to find examples of every stage of a stride which can then be placed in order. In one photograph of runners together in a race it is sometimes possible to find represented all the main stages of a typical running stride, which is helpful as the view and the lighting are then constant. More probably you will have to look at quite a large number of shots to find complete sets from several views.

To explain what you might be expected to cull from a reasonably full series of related photographs I refer you to the succession of drawings below (fig.1).

Starting from the left, the first two drawings are of stages of the running stride when both feet are off the ground. The body has been propelled forwards by the runner's left leg, the right leg is on the way to the ground for the next stride. In picture 3 contact with the ground has been made by the right leg which is slightly bent to absorb the shock of the body weight.

At the same time the left thigh is being swung

Fig.1

forward in preparation for the next stride, the lower leg and foot in typical flexion ready to be kicked downwards and forwards. As take-off from the right leg begins (4th drawing) the swing downwards of the left calf is initiated, until in the last drawing it is ready in its own turn to catch the weight of the body and pivot it forward over the contact point.

Side-to-side balance is beautifully maintained by weight shift from one side of the pelvis to the other, compensated by arm and shoulder movement. Notice how the right arm follows the left leg forward and vice-versa.

So it goes on, until the forward movement is arrested by a backward body lean and check steps. There are small variations dependent on personal style and speed. The smaller stride of jogging does not match the movement of a full sprint, but the basic action is universal.

Fig.2

Movement

Project 3

More collections of photographs are now needed, this time of clothed figures in vigorous action, which are rather less easy to come by.

What you should be hoping to find are instances where the violence or speed of the action has thrown or stretched the clothing into interesting or unpredictable shapes.

In the sporting field, there are some activities that are fairly well clothed; golf and cricket are examples in which normal clothing is spasmodically subjected to extreme stresses (figs.2 and 3).

Just copying the photographs without thought or selection will not help you to understand the action, as I have said, and with clothed figures there is the added need to understand the dynamics of the clothing. When drawing from pictures of golfers like these for example, you should look for the tense pulls in the cloth and draw them very firmly, concentrating more on their direction than on their every individual shape. Try to express the comparative slackness of rucked cloth by looser marks, almost letting the pencil feel its way loosely in your grasp in contrast to the firm incisive grip with which you make the stretched folds.

Fig.1 is a drawing resulting from analyses of three stages of a judo throw overlaid one over the other. The resultant pattern of shape has more movement in it than any one of the stages drawn on its own.

Fig.1

Fig.2

paper and *then* superimpose them. The final drawing can then be made from the arrangement that looks best.

How strongly each successive stage is drawn relatively to the others has to be a matter of judgement as the drawing progresses, in order to achieve a pattern of shapes and rhythms which best express the whole movement.

Lines of tension in clothing, for example, which are present in all the stages and whose shapes reinforce the direction of movement can be treated strongly, while detailed rendering of one peripheral part of one stage of the action might tend to arrest it.

Fig.3

If you are lucky enough to find a series of photographs like this, usually taken at 4 or 5 frames or more per second with a motor driven camera, you could try the same. Three successive actions are usually enough to cope with, especially if more than one figure is involved. It helps if there is one part of the action which remains fairly stable throughout the stages – a pivot point for example. This will then be drawn only once while the rest of the action is repeated one or more times, so providing the stable point about which the drawing will appear to rotate.

It is fairly difficult to superimpose stages by drawing direct, and much easier to make separate drawings of the stages on tracing

Composition

Composition as applied to drawing and painting is nothing more or less than the arrangement of the various elements of a picture on the drawing surface or within the frame.

Drawings, more often than not, do not completely cover the available picture area, but the untouched areas are nonetheless important elements in the composition. Every time you make a mark on an otherwise blank surface you make a start on a composition; the first line, by its placing establishes symmetry or assymmetry to what was immediately before featureless.

When placing a figure drawing on a sheet of paper you should always be conscious of the shapes and areas which are left untouched around it, and how they affect the 'balance' of the page.

Compositional balance is a hard thing to define. Absolute symmetry is clearly balanced and can be very satisfying, but it can also become boring and in any case the human figure is rarely seen symmetrically.

In abstract terms, if a main element, say a sitting figure, is moved away from the centre, it can be thought of as a weight tending to tip the picture about a central fulcrum. Depending on just where and what shape the figure is, the actual area of the larger space may be sufficient on its own to balance the off centre figure.

This concept is more difficult to accept and understand verbally than it is visually. The diagrams here clarify my meaning I hope. Fig.2(a) shows a seated figure placed to the left of the centre of a featureless background. The composition is reasonably satisfying, the shapes of figure and background area seeming to be acceptably balanced. There is however another factor contributing to the success of this arrangement which is underlined in fig.2(b), in which the same position in the composition is occupied by a left-to-right reversed version

of the figure. The reason why this looks unbalanced while the first one does not, is that the figure is facing out of the picture. Whichever way a figure is facing, and in a sense looking, the viewer's eye seems to be directed the same way, so that if it is towards the centre of the picture a larger space is felt to be satisfactory and necessary. When the figure is placed as in fig.2(b), the viewer's eye is led immediately out of the picture.

Fig.2(c), shows diagramatically the way that

Fig.1

Fig.2

an outward facing figure could be balanced by use of a large area of tone of medium weight. Smaller features of greater contrast can be made to do the same job rather more precariously (fig.2d).

It is almost impossible to be definitive about what is or is not a good composition. I can only introduce some of the elements that have to be considered and urge you to look analytically at the compositions of the past masters.

Composition

Project 1

It is always advisable to move around the model viewing the pose from several angles and eye levels before settling on your chosen viewpoint. So often I see a group of students in a life class, having established their places before the model has been posed, placidly accepting their view of the model without question.

While this is no doubt exemplary behaviour I think I would prefer a few minutes of mild chaos as everybody moved about and jockeyed for the best positions. Although it is true that there is something to be said for searching out the interest in a viewpoint that one is stuck with but would not normally have chosen, I think on balance it is better to find a view which strikes an immediate chord.

Hopefully in a fairly small group there will be room for some choice of viewpoint and I suggest that for this project you explore the compositional possibilities of one set-up from several different drawing positions. Don't forget that distance from the model and height of eye level are both variables to be added to the angle changes to produce different compositions.

Figs. 1 to 8, give some indication of the variety of compositions available from just one reclining pose on a bedstead, and these are only a few of the almost limitless variations.

If you are sharing the model with other students, they will frequently be in vision as you change your view of the model, in which case I think you should not hesitate to include them in your drawing. This does not mean that everything in your view should necessarily be included – you have the absolute right to reject and select at will to make the most exciting composition.

Aim to make at least two, preferably three or four compositional sketches in a two-hour period, which will require some pretty incisive and economical drawing if they are to be reasonably accurately organised. Obviously too much time must not be spent on the figure alone but it would be pointless to evolve a composition in which the figure lacked conviction.

Fig. 1

Fig.2

Fig.3

Fig.4

Fig.5

Fig.7

Fig.6

Fig.8

Fig.9

Composition

Project 2

Place the model in a cluttered situation so that the figure is only one of the many objects in view, not necessarily dominant or visible in entirety.

It is to be hoped that you may have acquired a few props in your studio by now, easels, boxes, lengths of material and the like. It is worth taking some time to create an environment for the model which is complex and varied in form and texture. The photographs here show views of the type of arrangement I have in mind, although they can be devised to render the figure even less conspicuous amongst a greater variety of objects. The limits on such compositions are set only by your ingenuity and the time available. One art school that I

visited recently had set up an environment of the most incredible complexity and richness of form. Objects as varied as musical instruments, animal skulls, garments, household utensils, were suspended on strings at various levels, and the model was posed in the middle. It took a day or two to devise and it was left up for two weeks or three weeks so that all the possibilities of juxtaposition of objects and figure could be explored.

If a suitable location is accessible to you and climate permits, it is worth doing a composition of this sort outdoors, where natural forms can be used to surround and partly obscure the model. (Fig.1.)

When drawing your own figure-enclosing environment, look as always, for composite patterns of shape. Parts of the set-up, however recognizable they may be as objects which, when separated, can have an entity of their

Fig.1

120

own, should be looked upon only as forms interacting with the whole.

Apertures through or between forms through which the figure can be seen, define the shape of the figure almost as a grid.

In the drawing, fig.3, an aluminium ladder frames the head and shoulders of the model, which makes a mini composition within the main one.

The shapes 'left' around the figure in this frame must be considered as carefully as those of the figure itself. Moreover the amount of her breast that is seen to the left of the ladder upright has to match what is seen and also be in the right position to link with the rest of the figure. For this to work, the *thickness* of the upright must be correct, and so on – every shape is dependent on and helps to define every other one. If one is wrong all are wrong, but there are so many cross-checking points and shapes, that if an honest, diligent search is made the whole thing will hold together and work as a total and satisfying interlocking pattern.

Fig.2

Fig.3

Composition

Project 3

I suggest that you now try some compositions in which space is a major element.

As it is essential to be able to get back some distance from the model, I realize that this could be a problem if only a small drawing studio is available.

If it is impossible to find the sort of space suggested by my composition, you could change venue, either as a group or singly, to a larger room, or even to an outdoor situation, weather permitting. It is not essential that the model should be nude for this exercise which should make it easier to arrange an alternative location.

The object of the exercise is to place the figure in a spacious environment in such a way that although the figure is a small element in the composition, it nevertheless commands attention.

One way to accomplish this is to place the figure absolutely in the centre of the picture with no competing areas of interest.

As I have said earlier, a symmetrical composition is fine if a still, ikon-like image is what you want. Otherwise try for slightly more testing asymmetric compositions.

The compositions shown here were both drawn in the life-drawing rooms of art schools, fig.2 in quite an old one, and the other in a very new college. In the older one, blue and grey painted wooden cupboards, boxes and tables mingled with plaster casts and other paraphernalia in a room dominated by pale grey and white walls.

By seating the model on top of the cupboards, high up in a corner, she was already in a focal point of interest in the composition. The model's throne and a box (or maybe it's a throne on its side) were placed to give more perspective lines leading to the figure, the cloth, feet, supporting table and pieces of plaster cast, adding incident to the corner in

Fig.1

122

contrast to the large plain shapes elsewhere.

In the other composition (fig.1), the life room is on the top floor of a modern block, surrounded by windows and largely furnished with steel and plastic cupboards, chairs and tables. There are traditional easels, 'donkeys' and a number of the usual props, but the overriding feeling on a bright day is of light and reflection.

I thought that the contrast of the wicker arm chair in which the model is curled, and the thin steel and plastic shapes of modern chair and table, linked by the concrete pillar, was interesting in itself, but the composition is really about light and dark shapes.

What this drawing reminds me that I liked and maybe could develop later in painting, is the interplay of the dart-like shape of light on the floor and wall, the harder shadows of the plastic chair back on the concrete pillar, the reflections in the right hand floor area and the lights and darks of the figure itself.

Fig.2

Composition

Project 4

Now move closer to the model to seek out compositions in which the figure is the dominating element.

Although it is possible to be some distance from the model and yet enlarge the figure to fill the picture area, it is generally not advisable, in my opinion.

For the reason why not, we have to consider another visual phenomenon.

When you look at a specific small object, your eye produces a clear sharp picture of that object *plus* a certain area of its surroundings. If your head is kept still, only this central area of vision is absolutely clear although *outside* it there is a much larger area of vision at the outer edges in which you can see movement and light but little else. The outer area of vision is designated peripheral, and the centre area is known as 60° cone of vision.

This cone is visualized in the diagram opposite. As you can see, the further away an object in a situation is, the more surrounding area is included in the cone of vision and the smaller the object becomes proportionately.

Now, there is a tacit assumption when viewing representational drawing or painting, or indeed photography, that the limits of the picture coincide approximately with the limits of the cone of vision. The photographer or the painter, in a sense, puts the viewer into the same position of view so that the complete scene is recreated.

If only part of the cone of vision is represented, or a lot more outside it, the effect is slightly strange and in extreme cases looks grossly distorted. The effect can be more clearly demonstrated by photography. A telephoto lens allows a photograph to be taken of a picture area which is only a small part of the unassisted cone of vision. When this part is enlarged to a normal picture, the perspective looks quite wrong, parallel lines seem not to be converging, and depth looks compressed. It is *not* in fact distorted, the perspective is absolutely correct, *for its original position in the cone of vision*. It looks wrong because the viewer assumes that it represents the complete cone of vision of a normal human eye, when it is in fact only a small, distant piece of it brought nearer by enlargement.

Conversely, a picture continued out of the cone of vision by drawing more and more of

Fig.1

the view seen as you turn to bring in new cones, will when viewed flat have a similarly curious appearance. Suppose, for example, that you begin a drawing looking down a straight road, gradually rotating until you are drawing the scene *across* the road and ultimately looking the *other* way down the same road. What happens to the line of the road? Its parallels will appear to converge to two vanishing points, one at each side of the picture, and it will *curve* across the centre. An extreme wide-angle lens, a fish eye so-called, does the same thing in photography. Both examples are extreme, but the principle still applies for lesser departures from the cone of vision.

So, unless there is a need for this rather special distortion, it is best to adjust your distance from the subject to fill your cone of vision i.e. move close in for compositions in which the figure looms large, very close if only a part of the figure is to be the subject, and move back for compositions which include more surroundings.

Fig.2

Fig.3

125

Composition

Project 5

In this project the aim is to produce compositions involving several figures, but to do this with the aid of only one model.

In addition to being economical in model fees, it is an interesting and useful exercise in that the composition evolves before your eyes in a way that cannot entirely be foreseen and may produce groupings which you would not have arrived at by any other means.

Preferably there should be sufficient room available for you to be able to position the model at discernibly different distances from your viewpoint – the greater the distances, the more variety of possible scale.

The procedure then is simply to pose the model in your chosen environment, draw this pose with particular care to relate it accurately to the surroundings and then to set up new poses in the same environment, adding them progressively to the same drawing.

The resulting figure composition is never actually seen in totality except in your drawing – the environment only ever actually contains one figure at a time.

It is obvious therefore, that the relationship between the figures cannot be checked as you draw – each figure has to be related carefully to the fixed surroundings, the figure *inter*-relationships only becoming evident as each new figure is added.

It may be necessary to complete parts of the environment covered by the first pose in order to place the second pose accurately, and indeed it may sometimes be considered preferable to draw the environment completely before adding the figures.

For example, in fig. 2, the figures were posed in and on a scaffolding tower which has a dominating coherent structure of its own to which the figures must conform, and which could have been drawn completely and accurately before the figures were added, thereby also performing the function of a grid to help fix the poses. It is not necessary to do it this way though – in such a case each figure can be drawn in its immediate area by observing the interplay between its shape and the framing bars and the spaces, so evolving scaffolding and figures together.

Fig.1

126

Drawing quickly and simply with charcoal will allow you to explore a number of compositional variations in this way, some of which may suggest groupings which can be contrived and studied rather more penetratingly on later sessions.

There is no reason, for instance, why a composite drawing should not be continued through several sessions, a carefully observed figure being added in each session to a carefully retained identical situation.

Be careful to ensure that succeeding poses do not occupy some of the same spatial volume as a previous pose, which would result in a feeling of unreality without convincing depth.

I feel bound to say that there are many visually fascinating possibilities resulting from multiple figure drawings which are intentionally *not* arranged to occupy space in a 'real' way, but then this is not strictly objective drawing and has moved beyond the declared compass of this particular study.

Fig.2

Creativity

We come now to an area that is rather difficult to define.

Until now I have been discussing ways of improving observation in order to make more and more incisive studies of the human form and I have stressed the need to search for information about reality and to record the discoveries in an economical and selective way. I consider this searching out and gathering in of information to be fundamental to objective drawing.

At its most basic level it can be thought of as the energizing and refuelling process for the creativity which is to follow.

Of course it is never quite so clear cut as this; each artist, however like a blank slate he tries to be, brings to observation some emotional response which colours even the most austere information gathering.

It is at the point where the artist turns away from the model, having seen and collated enough from direct observation and wants the emotional response now to be given freedom, that I think the emphasis changes from objective to creative.

Sometimes the transition from one to the other can be almost instantaneous, where information is taken in, emotionally processed and then given out in a variety of forms which may have little obvious objective resemblance to the original.

Letting a method or a medium have its head can sometimes provide the catalyst which pushes an objective study into the area of creativity. Similarly extreme selectivity in use of the discovered shapes can produce near abstractions.

My painting/drawing here is I suppose a bit of both. Certainly I was interested in the interplay of shapes in the figure and those on the floor, tables and walls, but the particular way that the washes took to the rough water colour paper had a lot to do with the decision to leave the shapes and forms so minimal.

Another way to influence the output is consciously to manipulate the input i.e. to change the real object by various devices *before* drawing it objectively. A few ways of doing this are described in the first project of this section.

Perhaps the whole creative idea will come from the imagination or from a desire to give form to a story or myth. The objective drawings may then be made purely to be used as reference material to populate the imaginary composition.

There are so many, many ways to extend drawing into increasingly esoteric areas of creativity that it would be impossible here to do more than suggest a few directions to begin exploring.

The following projects are intended to do just that.

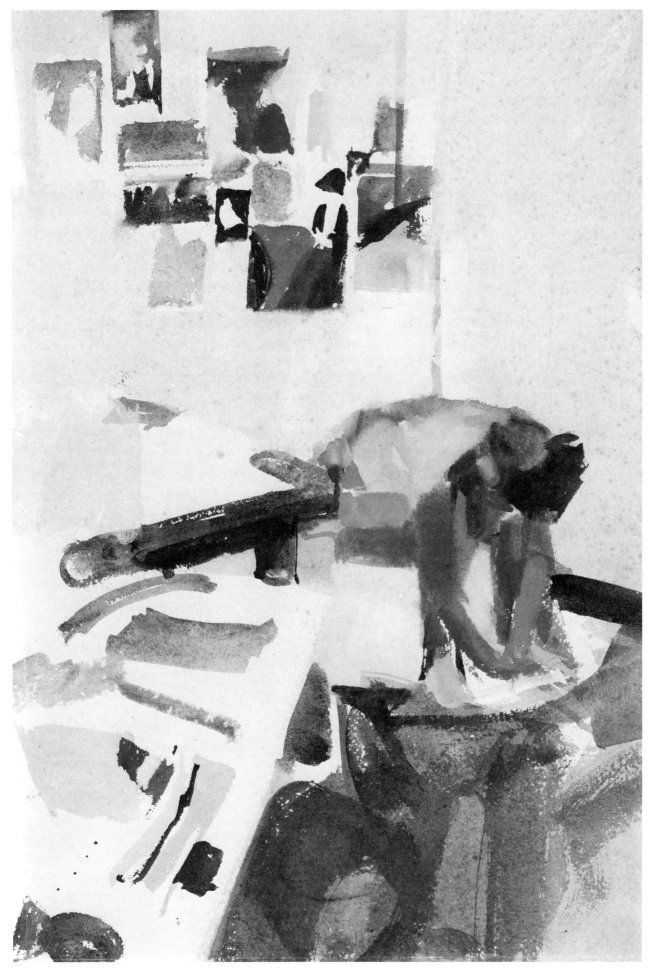

Fig.1

Creativity

Project 1

Construct a complete situation for the model based on a particular composition or the general style of an established master.

Here are a few suggestions.

Find a reproduction of Manet's *Olympia* (which was itself based on *The Venus of Urbino* by Titian) and base a composition on it. Find fabric and pillows to make up a couch or bed in a similar way, pose your model similarly and draw the whole as a possible variation on the theme. The background figure could either be copied, or posed by the same model later, or even substituted by a vase of flowers or other decoration.

A Francois Boucher type of composition could be simulated if you have a young, reasonably pretty girl as a model. A typical Boucher would be a rather exhuberantly decorative pose with rich surroundings of drapery and bric-a-brac.

In many of his paintings Gustav Klimt nearly submerged the figures in boldly patterned fabrics, flatly represented. A set up of this type was the basis of my water colour drawing here (fig.1), which in black-and-white reproduction may very well conceal the figure even more than it does in the colour original. It is not absolutely necessary to draw these highly patterned compositions in colour, but it does help. The background fabric in this drawing is basically yellow with orange and purple decoration, the fabric wrapped around the figure is green, figured with blue and purple and there are tints and shades of these colours in the figure and around. Many of these colours are tonally undifferentiated and would merge if drawn in black-and-white, where a tonal value of grey must be allocated to represent every colour. It can be done and it can be interesting but it decreases the range of pattern possibilities.

You could try a Matisse *Odalisque* composition, of which he painted several, the name meaning 'female slave in a harem', although they are sometimes entitled *Decorative figure on an ornamental background*.

A 'captured instant' composition of the type inspired by documentary photography and exploited by Degas and Vuillard can be interesting to simulate. A bathed-in-light patterned domestic interior may not be beyond your ingenuity to create, à la Bonnard. There will be many other paintings and artists that will spark off ideas for situations that you can create which are rich and exciting.

Having spent some time making such an arrangement, it will be something of a waste to use it only for a two- or three-hour session. If you or your group can manage to find a few days or a week to extend the drawing into a painting, perhaps on canvas or a primed board, it will be found to be really worthwhile. It is amazing how much progress can be made in the understanding of figure drawing and painting in a concentrated period of a few days, as opposed to two-hourly sessions once a week.

Fig.1

Fig.2

Creativity

Project 2

Another completely different method of modifying reality before drawing involves the use of light, either generated or natural.

It only needs an ordinary 35mm slide projector, some empty slide holders and a few slide-size pieces of clear acetate, to provide almost infinite variations of patterns of light on your model.

Some clear acetates take pen lines or colour better than others – it is usually possible nowadays to obtain pads of clear film specifically designed to take ink and paint without problems. 'Artcel' and 'Drawfilm' are two current product names in this country. The thickness should be about the same as photographic film; very thin kitchen cellophane is no good.

Having found a suitable acetate film, draw a few simple patterns on it in areas equivalent to the picture area of the 35mm slide holder. Very simple regular patterns usually yield the best results, so initially at least, keep to various width and colour parallel lines or square grids. Fix the grids into the slide holders and load them into the projector-carrier.

When these slides are projected onto the

Fig.1

132

Fig.2

model in a fairly dark room, the most interesting linear patterns result as the projected grids are bent and twisted by the forms of the figure. Every change of position of the projector relative to the model results in a whole new set of patterns and the permutations are fascinating to observe.

Two problems have to be overcome in order to draw these patterns however. Firstly any change in the pose, however small, alters the projected patterns; even the model's breathing is revealed by a close textured regular grid, so it is essential to choose a pose where movement can be kept to the minimum.

Secondly, light for the drawing boards is hard to come by without drowning out the projected patterns. There will be some reflected light from walls, and a few shaded and carefully directed angle-poise lamps should do the trick, and you will probably have to adapt to drawing in more subdued lighting than usual.

The pencil drawing (fig.2) is a record of the result of projecting a slide of the union jack from a low central position in front of the model. Colours and shadow areas are labelled by numerals, No.1 denoting blue areas, No.2 red, and No.3 areas of total shadow.

Creativity

Project 3

As an extension of the last project in which lines were generated on the surfaces *before* drawing, I suggest that, with the patterns that you saw still in your mind, you return to drawing with line but using a line which makes its own patterns.

Choose a black ineradicable medium such as pen and ink, fine felt or fibre-tip pen, rapidograph or similar. Having set any pose which, from the previous projects, has been found to be interesting and worthy of further study, draw with an almost continuous line.

Let the pen wander over the forms, not following exterior outlines only, but wandering almost randomly over the surfaces as though describing the track of a fly as it clambers over the forms.

As you feel your way over the forms, try to sense the planes with the pen tip, almost as though you were running your finger tips over the surfaces with your eyes closed. You may begin to produce lines which surround high forms and proliferate in the hollows, like a computer-generated contour map.

Maybe your line-trailing fly will be attracted to the junctions of light and shade, in which case the wandering line may begin to build up a suggestion of tonality and illuminated form. The aim is to be watching and only loosely in control of a continuous series of random responses to intense observation. It has been called 'taking a line for a walk', and it can produce surprising results. At the very least it may free you from the tyranny, if you are still subject to it, of the linear outline.

The wandering line may actually ignore the outside edge of the figure altogether in places, and later on some tones may be filled in for no other reason than that it seems to make the pattern more interesting.

Another variation of the procedure is to look at the pose and before you start drawing, 'see' it in terms of a linear pattern. Draw that pattern only and then stop. Drawings figs.1 and 4, were of this type and fig.1 was more or less accidently wetted later which blurred the non-waterproof fibre pen line and I thought rather improved the pattern.

Fig.1

134

Fig.2

Fig.3

Fig.4

135

Creativity

Project 4

This last project has really just brought us to the beginning of the activity which has been the main motivation of drawing for centuries – that is original composition, for which drawings or studies are made.

Drawings were originally self sufficient perhaps, but since the Italian Renaissance at least, the primary function of figure drawing has been to gather information from life for use in figure compositions.

We now value many of these drawings as works of art in their own right, but they were only intended as working drawings. More recently, especially since the advent of printing, drawings have increasingly been made for their own sake, but the function of drawings as studies still remains relevant.

Moreover the necessity to record information which can be made use of later in a painting, makes sure that the drawing really does say something useful. A superficially pretty

drawing which is fundamentally unsound is impossible to work from.

Reproduced here is a compositional scheme for a group portrait. Before this stage is reached a few or perhaps more than a few compositional ideas have been considered on a smaller scale, perhaps as thumbnail sketches, very abstract. One of these ideas is then developed further to determine more precisely the abstract relationship of the figures with all the other elements and areas. Some sketches may be made or polaroid photographs taken at this stage to confirm how much of the imagined grouping is possible. For further development as either a drawing or a painting, studies of the individual figures and other single elements can be made in poses and lighting as required by the overall compositional plan.

As the finished work progresses, figures may not work in the composition as well as you hope, and new studies may be made which in turn suggest new groupings and so on. Some elements of a painting are changed many times and require a large number of studies before final decisions are made.

Fig.1

Such drawings may be absolutely straightforward and ordinary but they should be workmanlike, and they are truly an essential part of a creative process.

Drawings can go much further than this though – as I said at the beginning, this is a book about objective figure drawing. Once you can draw well (and you can always draw better) there is a large range of possible ways of experimenting with figure drawing, to which this section is merely an introduction.

Maybe those possibilities will be explored in my next book!

Fig.3

Fig.2

Master drawings

This final section of the book looks at the work of some of the great masters of figure drawing, and attempts to demonstrate some connections between their works and the main themes that I have been discussing in this book. In the limited space available, I am obviously not able to provide anything like a thorough history of figure drawing, and have chosen, fairly arbitrarily, some works that I particularly liked or found interesting. As well as practising your own drawing, you should take every opportunity to look at the works of the masters, and think about what it is that they have achieved in making an especially successful, or especially beautiful, drawing: you may notice things that you would never have seen on your own, or realize how a great artist has found a simple solution to a problem that has been confusing you for a long time. There are many great names in figure drawing; in addition to the ones whose work is illustrated here, I have also to mention Leonardo, Michelangelo, Botticelli, Dürer, El Greco, Raphael, Caravaggio, Rubens, Rembrandt and Velasquez, among the old masters, and Ingres, Degas, Millet, Eakins, Lautrec, Modigliani, Picasso, Pascin and Wyeth as more modern artists. They have all drawn the human figure with sensitivity and understanding.

The drawings in this final section are arranged very roughly in chronological order, but I have also been concerned to put together works that could usefully be compared or contrasted with each other.

The first work shown is a copy by the little-known draughtsman Giorgio Guilio Clovio (1498-1578), of a lost drawing of a Pietà by Michelangelo. It is very subtly drawn, probably in black chalk, and the plasticity of the flesh in the figure of Christ is beautifully expressed; look for instance at the way the flesh of Christ's right arm is squashed as it rests on the knee of Mary. Apart from this figure, there is very little sense of real three-dimensional depth or solidity, as the artist has concentrated rather on the compositional pattern of the work. There is instead a fascinating interplay of the folded patterns of the cloth, the undulating surface of the figure of Christ and the gesturing hands of the other figures. It is clear that, whatever was the emphasis of Michelangelo's lost original, Clovio's work is a study in pattern and composition more than about space and light.

By comparison, the sketch of Sir Thomas More and his family by Hans Holbein (1497-1543) is not so much a compositional scheme as a diagram, a stage on the way to a painting, exploring the proposed figure placings. The sketch gives no indication of light and shade, and, since the finished work was destroyed by fire, we do not know how the tonal balance was organized.

Despite this lack of tonality and weightiness, it is apparent that the figure of More himself dominates the work. He is, in fact, virtually at the centre of the composition. This feeling of dominance is if anything heightened by the comparative simplicity of his figure; the only texture is supplied by the detail of his chain of office, which itself draws attention to his face, with its rapt and concentrated gaze.

Drawing of the Pieta by Giorgio Guilio Clovio after a drawing by Michelangelo, a beautiful composition with a well-observed drawing of the central figure of Christ. Victoria and Albert Museum, London.

A sketch by Hans Holbein for a painting of Sir Thomas More and his family, drawn in 1526. Though intended as a working drawing, it is an excellent study in the creative use of line. Kunstmuseum, Basel.

Probably, to judge from other surviving works by Holbein, the shapes of the various garments would have been organized into closely related tones, to draw further attention to the heads of the sitters. Even so, in this drawing the pattern and texture of simple linear outlines creates a decoration which is none the less splendid for being a minor aspect of the final work, or even perhaps being an unintentional achievement.

The back view of a male draped figure on page 142 is a study by the Venetian painter Tintoretto (1518-94) for the figure of the landlord in his painting of the Last Supper which he did in San Paulo, Venice, in the late 1560s. This drawing is appealing in its directness and unity. While it yields some information about the fall of light on the figure, the artist's primary interest seems to lie in the folding and stretching of the simple garment, which manages to evoke the pose of the figure beneath with certainty and conviction.

The nervous, knotted figure is also by Tintoretto, and, like the previous drawing, is drawn on grey paper with black chalk, although this time there are no white highlights. It is thought to have been a study from a piece of sculpture representing a man bowed down with a heavy burden, possibly the mythological figure of Atlas. It is also an excellent example of the flickering, mannerist style of an artist who tried to emulate and adapt the achievements in draughtsmanship of Michelangelo to his visionary view of the world. The forms are convoluted in a way that they could never be in life, but they are strangely convincing and expressive, and give to the work an extraordinary life and vitality. Most of the bumps and hollows have a soundly observed anatomical explanation, and the way in which the outline has an exaggerated weariness gives a marvellous impression of tottering under a heavy weight. Some of the marks may seem out of place and these are stains that have appeared since the sixteenth century.

It might be interesting to compare these works with the back view of a half-clothed male by Nicholas Lancret in the early eighteenth century. Though drawn 150 years later than the Tintorettos, this displays an equivalent simplicity and conviction; the

A back view of a draped male figure by Tintoretto, one of the most original figure draughtsmen of the Renaissance. This study explores the definition of the underlying form purely in terms of the folding and stretching of the drapery. Victoria and Albert Museum, London.

Another figure by Tintoretto, combining his heightened, dramatic view of man with his interest in dynamics. Victoria and Albert Museum, London.

Standing figure of a man by Nicholas Lancret, a pupil of Antoine Watteau, combining robust observation with an elegance typical of the Rococo. Museum Boymano-van Beuningen, Rotterdam.

stylistic differences between the finished works of the two masters are not at all apparent in their working drawings.

The next two drawings are much more modern. First, a typically rich drawing of a standing nude by the post-impressionist painter Georges Seurat (1859-91). It is primarily done in conté crayon, but on close examination it is possible to see a much lighter grey underdrawing, perhaps in pencil. Seurat's work is wonderful for the organization of its tonality; even the brightest of the highlights has a little tone. Although it may not be visible in reproduction, the hip, for instance, carries a delicate, spidery tracery of conté lines, and this becomes stronger and thicker on the lesser lights. As a study in tone it is completely uncompromising – there is no edge line to the figure at all. The hands and feet simply disappear into the background gloom, yet there is overall a splendid feeling of solidity and atmosphere. It may be interesting to compare this drawing with the points I raised in the section on Light and Shade, projects 1 and 4.

The reclining nude by the modern British artist Victor Pasmore (*b.* 1908) is more overtly sexual. It is not, of course, a drawing but one of the two or three paintings I have included for their strict selectivity or for the strong evidence of draughtsmanship. Where the Seuret was a study in direct light, this explores a more complex interplay of direct and reflected light. The structure of the back is simple, and the composition gives depth and atmosphere, but the subtlety of the lighting continually draws your attention back to the delicious fleshy and ovoid shape of the hip and bottom. I suppose it could be called titillating; but it is wonderfully done.

Pages 146 and 147 compares standing clothed female figures by two very different artists, the Viennese *art nouveau* painter Gustav Klimt (1862-1918), and the British portrait painter Augustus John (1879-1961). Klimt was fascinated by flat patterns, which he has explored in the drapery of his figure; yet the evocation of the pose is extremely vivid here. He has managed, with the barest minimum of pencil strokes, to indicate without question that the model's weight is on her left leg, and to show the swing of her torso, the way in which her left shoulder is tilted down and

143

144

Reclining nude by Victor Pasmore. Another study in light and shade, but one which also frankly delights in the textures of the flesh. Tate Gallery, London.

her head is counterbalanced. He has also included the hint of exotic mystery in the pose which is characteristic of his art. Equally fine, and also by Klimt, is the study of two reclining nudes; the undulating, flowing line captures the sensuality, and the slackness of the form that were discussed in the section on Dynamics.

The work by Augustus John, of his wife Dorelia John, was done in pencil and water-colour. The pose is strong and balanced, and although the fabric of the dress falls cleanly to the ground, it contrives to suggest the pose underneath. As in the Klimt, the weight is on the left leg. Where the Klimt emphasized flat pattern, this drawing has the form shown with added tone. The tension and weight of the cloth are shown in strong straight lines, while the fold of the cloth at the elbow is freely expressed. The head is nicely inclined to counterbalance the pose, and contrives to suggest a totally different character to the Klimt. Both of these works might usefully be compared with the sections on Balance and Clothing.

Opposite: Standing figure by the French Post-Impressionist Georges Seurat. He carried out scientific studies of tonal systems which formed the basis for his pointillist style of painting, and this interest in tone is evident in such careful, entirely non-linear drawings. Courtauld Institute Galleries, London.

Study for the mythological figure of Hygieia by Gustav Klimt, a study in flat patterns which nevertheless reveals an exactly balanced pose. Victoria and Albert Museum, London.

Opposite: Dorelia standing, by the British artist Augustus John, a study in the tensions and slacknesses of clothing contrasting the tight bodice and full skirting and adding up to a charming pose. City of Manchester Art Galleries.

Study for two reclining female nudes, also by Klimt. The art nouveau lines explore the relaxed flesh and bones of the model. Victoria and Albert Museum, London.

This next spread looks at studies and compositional sketches for paintings by the English Pre-Raphaelite Dante Gabriel Rossetti (1828-82) and the contemporary English artist David Hockney (*b.* 1937). The sketch for Hockney's large painting *Mr & Mrs Clark and Percy* explores the relationships between the characters and the composition of the whole work. Incidentally, as Percy the cat, which features in Ossie Clark's lap in the final work, is here missing, the title to the painting must have been chosen at a later stage. Hockney did a great many studies for this painting, and took many photographs, and he has admitted that he found great difficulty with the portrait of Mr Clark. The pencil sketch here is very similar to the head finally used in the painting, but the body has a completely different pose. Unusually for Hockney, both the figures in this work look straight out and establish eye-to-eye contact with the viewer. Admittedly these two drawings are not masterpieces in their own right, but they are good examples of real working drawings.

The Rossetti drawings show a rather different

Two studies by Dante Gabriel Rossetti for a never-completed painting, demonstrating a different, more detailed, method of working from Hockney's. Birmingham Museum and Art Gallery.

Opposite top and bottom: Two studies by David Hockney for his painting Mr and Mrs Clark and Percy, *working drawings that demonstrate the importance of composition in Hockney's portraiture. Tate Gallery, London.*

emphasis, and different method of working, typical of the Pre-Raphaelites' prediliction for pictures that tell a story, and the requirement of their creed to depict every little detail with 'truth' and 'clarity'. Like the Hockney, the subjects of these studies for an unknown painting are seen against the light source, and where Hockney concentrates on the compositional pattern, Rossetti has paid much more attention to the way the light falls on the figures. It was a common practice of Rossetti and his associates to make nude studies for the clothed figures; the drapery being added so that it clung to the figure, revealed almost as much as it concealed and yet remained superficially pure and chaste. In this case, I

think it unlikely that such a sexually desirable figure was intended and so I think it probable that a draped study of this figure would have been made as well and information from the two combined for the painting.

The painting by the Swiss sculptor Alberto Giacometti (1901-66) seems to have begun as a study of a seated figure and ended up as a strangely concentrated image of a human face. Giacometti primarily produced thin sculpted figures, and here the head has begun to take on the compressed form that is typical of his work; although it will not be apparent in black-and-white reproduction, the painting has even got the colour and sheen of a bronze casting. The artist has obviously made a search for the form of the body, as can be seen in the network of lines, ticks and scrubbed tone, but it is apparent that his attention was drawn again and again to the head. The intensity of his search for form in that region is such that it not only takes on a strong sense of being in the round, but seems almost to be in an atmosphere and space of its own.

Where the Giacometti has sacrificed the individuality of the sitter, the portrait of P J Spencer by the English artist Stanley Spencer (1891-1959) has concentrated on portraying the character of the sitter by seeking out the uniqueness of his face. The portrait is typical of Spencer's work in its interest in the localized asymmetries of the details of the flesh of the face, such as the slightly one-sided nose and eyes which are marginally different in shape. Such asymmetries are to be found in most faces, and Spencer's portrait is notable for its exploration of these without any disturbance of the general symmetry of the whole. This is achieved because he has been able to ensure that the details, such as the folds and undulations of the skin, are not allowed to disturb the strong feeling for the general planes. This drawing is typical of the artist's work also in that the forms are absolutely continuous, and no area of the head is skimped or left unstated.

Portrait of P. J. Spencer by Stanley Spencer, a drawing of great subtlety which achieves tonal and structural strength and still manages to pay attention to the idiosyncrasies of the flesh. Tate Gallery, London.

Opposite: Caroline by Giacometti, a painted sketch which has become a portrait; the strong sense of form in the head reflects the artist's sculptural interests. Tate Gallery, London.

The standing figure on page 152 is a study by Pierre-Auguste Renoir (1841-1919) for his painting of *Les Grandes Baigneuses* (1884-87). It is a beautifully strong and simple drawing, bursting with youth and vitality. The figure has great solidity and weight, the tautness of the form around the shoulder-blades seems to me to imbue the whole curve of the spine with a kind of tensed springiness. The angle of the head is just right, and the whole figure is of a piece. In my view this drawing is much more unified, more alive and more successful than the figure in the finished painting, and an excellent illustration of dynamics in drawing.

Like the Renoir, the drawing by Egon Schiele (1890-1918) is a study of a girl's back; but

152

Back view of a female nude by Egon Schiele, a painful but fascinating study of the structure of the body. Graphische Sammlung Albertina, Vienna.

Opposite: Sketch by Pierre Auguste Renoir for his painting Les Grandes Baigneuses, *a vigorous drawing which strongly reveals the artist's control of the dynamics of the figure.*

beyond that, there is no similarity at all between the two works. Schiele's eye is merciless. The almost painful boniness and meanness of the flesh is heightened by the elongation of the torso. The drawing was made on buff-coloured paper, and the artist has used this as the intermediate tone for the figure, heightening the lights with watercolour and gouache. To help clarify the place of the paper's colour in the tonality of the figure, he has isolated it from the background by painting white gouache to delineate the edge of the figure. As well as assisting in using the paper's colour as a ready-made tone, this device also dramatizes the outline shape.

What is not apparent in the black-and-white reproduction here is the way in which smudges of pink and blue are used to accentuate knuckles and joints, and pale acid green and yellow to help round out the fuller forms. Although at first sight these colours usually seem harsh and shocking, I always feel that they contribute perfectly to the overall sense of vitality.

Because I feel that familiarity with Schiele's drawing should be a high priority for anyone interested in figure drawing, I have included two more of his works, *Recumbent nude girl with her legs apart* and the *Man with a red loin cloth* of 1914.

The female figure is typical of his ability to convey a great deal with the minimum of means. The underlying skeleton is always prominent, and line is used to delineate the skeletal structure whenever it comes to the surface. But the linear outline is expressive, and with the linear definition of the edges of the forms, and the small smudges conveying tone, this is a drawing of extraordinary intensity.

The small areas of tone are so few as merely to emphasize the uncompromising directness of the linear treatment, which, though spare, manages to convey sensuously the hardness and softness of the figure. Notice, incidentally, the foreshortening of the model's right thigh has been simply achieved with two loosely ovoid shapes, and the other thigh is made marvellously lucid by similar means.

To add to the eloquence of the line in these drawings, Schiele would blur the line subtly towards the swelling of the form, sometimes by

Above and left: Recumbent nude girl with her legs apart, *and* Man with a red loin cloth, *both by Schiele. Both are excellent illustrations of the use of line in the study of the dynamics of the figure, and an original method of portraying character. Graphische Sammlung Albertina, Vienna.*

Opposite: Naked portrait by Lucien Freud, an uncompromisingly honest study which maintains a strong sense of structure and composition. Tate Gallery, London.

smudging the chalk, but more often by adding small amounts of water-colour or gouache.

Although it is not apparent from the title, I suspect that the male drawing is one of Schiele's many self-portraits. It is hard to see how he managed to draw it in such a pose, but there is a similar difficulty with many of his acknowledged self-portraits; this pose could have been drawn from the mirror until it was necessary to observe the arm over the head (the artist's right arm). He would have had to hold this arm up to observe it in the mirror, then move it to do the actual drawing.

In this work, the convolutions of the linear

outlines have been pushed beyond any possible objective reality, but all the shapes are based on observation and their exaggeration is just enough to heighten the feeling of tension in bone and muscle which gives the drawing such tortured intensity.

The next two works are by contemporary British painters, Lucien Freud (*b.* 1922) and Euan Uglow (*b.* 1932). Both are, of course, paintings but could be considered as drawings in paint. The Freud includes some extremely subtle colour changes which are lost in reproduction but which modulate between describing the changing colour of the skin's

surface and the light and shade to help define form.

But I have included the painting here primarily because it is structurally so strong, not only compositionally but in terms of the figure itself, and the figure's relationship with the flat plane of the bed. And like all of Freud's work, it is uncompromisingly honest and un-idealized, almost cruel in its observation: nothing is sensationalized or hidden.

It is also (although I cannot be sure of how high a priority the artist gave this) a very well organized exercise in light and shade, without any dramatic shadow or highlighting.

*Female nude, by Auguste Rodin, a rapid sketch of a fleeting
moment, made in the attempt to capture total movement.
Victoria and Albert Museum, London.*

*Opposite: Seated nude by Euan Uglow, an exercise in
structure so complete that the figure and chair almost
merge into a single, coherent, form. Tate Gallery, London.*

The seated nude by Uglow, done in 1962-63, is equally strong structurally, and indeed much has been sacrificed in the search for the planes. The vertical tip of the head, the parallel planes of the forward-facing shoulders and of the knees are all blocked in with very strong lines (bright red in the original) and there is no attempt to soften these original statements or to make the transitions smoother or more flesh-like. The chair-legs and the model's feet all stand solid on the floor, the plane of which is beyond doubt. Although I am sure that the painting succeeds in capturing the character of the sitter, it is not a genuine portrait with real human presence as is the Freud, and you feel that the light is only there to illuminate the structure.

Pages 157 and 158 compare two very different drawings by the sculptors August Rodin (1840-1917) and Henry Moore (*b*. 1898) Rodin was concerned to explore the human figure in rapid motion, and he used to draw with great speed from models who were encouraged to move freely about his room. He was searching for the 'expressive line', the single bodily gesture that expressed everything about the figure and even about humanity. His drawings are as a result about fluidity of movement and vitality. As in this example, he often used to fill the flowing outlines with freely applied washes of colour. These made no attempt to depict light or form, but somehow they continue to imbue the figures with a degree of fleshy solidity.

The reclining nude by Henry Moore, by contrast, has the effect of an almost rock-like solidity and weight. It, too, was drawn fluidly and rapidly, but it shows the figure as a powerful landscape. This difference between the formal preoccupations of the two great artists can be seen equally clearly in their finished sculptures: Rodin's figures seem to defy gravity while Moore's glory in their weightiness.

Conclusion

Looking at drawings by great artists is, I repeat, very important and necessary to the aspiring figure draughtsman.

Given limitless time and diligence, everything about drawing can be discovered entirely on your own without help, but the whole point is that there is not sufficient time in a life time to discover everything, and without guidance an awful lot of blind alleys will have to be explored, too many trials and too much error.

Climb onto the shoulders of the draughtsmen who have gone before and get a clearer view.

Reclining nude by Henry Moore, in which the artist has concentrated on the weightiness of the figure to such an extent that the result is almost topographical. Victoria and Albert Museum, London.

Bibliography

The Art Of Drawing, Richard Kenin, Paddington Press.

Experimental Drawing, Robert Kaupelis, Pitman Publishing Ltd.

Drawing: A Study Guide, Daniel M. Mendelowitz, Holt Rinehart Winston (1967).

Drawing, Seeing And Observation, Ian Simpson, Von Nostrand Reinhold.

Human Anatomy And Figure Drawing, Jack N. Kramer, Von Nostrand Reinhold.

Atlas Of Human Anatomy For The Artist, Stephen Rogers Peck, Oxford University Press, New York (1951).

Grammar Of Drawing For Artists And Designers, Colin Hayes, Studio Vista and Von Nostrand Reinhold (1969).

Human Anatomy For The Artist, John Raynes, Hamlyn.

The Nude, Kenneth Clark, John Murray Ltd.

Egon Schiele, Alessandro Comini, Thames & Hudson (1976).

Watercolours And Drawings of Egon Schiele, Thames & Hudson (1970).

Master Draughtsman Series, Borden Publishing Company, California.

Acknowledgements

Photographs

Graphische Sammlung Albertina, Vienna 153, 154 top, 154 bottom; British Museum, London 8; City Art Gallery, Manchester 147; City Museum and Art Gallery, Birmingham 11, 12; Courtauld Institute of Art, London 144; Durand-Ruel & Cie, Paris 152; Hamlyn Group Picture Library 7 top, 146 bottom; Hirmer Verlag, Munich 7 bottom; Kodak Museum, Harrow 110–111; Kunstmuseum, Basel 140–141; Kupferstichkabinett, Preussischer Kulturbesitz, Berlin 9; Metropolitan Museum of Art, New York 7 centre; Museum Boymans-von Beuningen, Rotterdam 143; Philadelphia Museum of Art, Pennsylvania 111; Roger-Viollet, Paris 6; Tate Gallery, London 145, 148 top, 148 bottom, 150, 151, 155, 156; Victoria and Albert Museum, London 139, 142 left, 142 right, 146 top, 157, 158.

© A.D.A.G.P. Paris, 1981, 111, 150.

The photographs reproduced on pages 48, 61, 62 to 63, 64 to 65, 118 to 119 and 121 were all provided by the author.

The drawings reproduced on page 148 ($17 \times 13\frac{7}{8}$ inches and $10\frac{5}{8} \times 15\frac{7}{8}$ inches) are © David Hockney, 1970, Courtesy Petersburg Press.